Ram Barkai was born in 1957 in a little Kibbutz by the Sea of Galilee, Israel to Ruth and Meyer from Romania. Ram left high school in 1974 to explore social work in north Israel before he joined the army in 1985. Ram spent five years in the army and left in 1980 to travel and study. He was discharged as a Major. Ram enrolled in the Science university in Haifa to study computer science with a strong flavour of math. In 1987 Ram left Israel for Japan to work in computers and later on in finance. Ram came back to South Africa in 1996 to settle down and build a home with his first wife. He joined a small financial services company and became the CEO in 2005. Ram retired in 2012 to pursue his real passion for Ice Swimming, which he founded in 2009. Ram completed many swims around the world, from the Arctic, Antarctica, Dead Sea, Cape Point, Cape Horn, Siberia, Alaska, Patagonia, Australia, Murmansk, Finland, Norway, Yellow River China, Sea of Galilee and many more in frozen Europe, England, Ireland & Scotland.

All records are available on www.openwaterpedia.com/wiki/Ram_Barkai and longswims.com/p/ram-barkai/. Ram holds five Guinness World Records, and many Ice-Swimming records and has been inducted into the Ice Swimming Hall of Fame as a Swimmer and an Administrator. Ram completed 11 Ice Miles around the world and 17 Ice Km as well as many shorter ice swims. Ram is a father to four children whom he calls my fantastic four. Ram lives with Sam wonder-woman his partner in Cape Town.

To my fantastic four: Kaitlin, Jordan, Gilad and Neve, you made my life whole.

Ram Barkai

From Fire to Ice

1-Oct-2022

Dear Laure,

Enjoy the story
&
See you in the
ICE

Ram Barkai

Austin Macauley Publishers
LONDON • CAMBRIDGE • NEW YORK • SHARJAH

Copyright © Ram Barkai 2022

The right of Ram Barkai to be identified as the author of this work has been asserted by the author in accordance with sections 77 and 78 of the Copyright, Designs and Patents Act 1988.

All rights reserved. No part of this publication may be reproduced, stored in a retrieval system, or transmitted in any form or by any means, electronic, mechanical, photocopying, recording, or otherwise, without the prior permission of the publishers.

Any person who commits any unauthorised act in relation to this publication may be liable to criminal prosecution and civil claims for damages.

All of the events in this memoir are true to the best of the author's memory. The views expressed in this memoir are solely those of the author.

A CIP catalogue record for this title is available from the British Library.

ISBN 9781528979931 (Paperback)
ISBN 9781398423107 (Hardback)
ISBN 9781398423114 (ePub e-book)

www.austinmacauley.com

First Published 2022
Austin Macauley Publishers Ltd®
1 Canada Square
Canary Wharf
London
E14 5AA

Acknowledgments

I'm a storyteller when the moment is right. I don't talk much, or I talk a lot. Nothing in my life was a middle ground. I never followed a specific mentor, but I listen all the time and learnt from so many people around me. I didn't mention many names because I am not good at balancing this and many, I simply can't remember their exact names. So many people were part of my journey that trying to acknowledge each one would have gotten me utterly lost. I do, however, want to use this chapter to thank you all.

Thank you to my parents, Ruth and Meyer and my amazing brothers, Hemi, Amos and Yair, and their extended family. I even thank my ex-wives, Kim and Nadine who gave me wonderful kids and nearly bankrupt me twice. I learnt most from my kids. Seeing them growing up and developing into adults, forming from a little miracle that materialised from 'nowhere' into a person with personality, opinions, values and love. Kaitlin, Jordan, Gilad and Neve, you inspired me the most. Many of my friends from childhood; Itai, my childhood best friend and friend for life, Offer, with whom we shared some crazy high school and army adventures, who passed away from cancer, many others in the army, university and travels who moved on in life and lost contact, Omri and Jeremy and many more, thank you all for inspiring me. To my place of birth, Kibbutz Ma'agan where I discovered life and water. Thank you all.

Later in my swimming and ice life, The MLPs, we did have some amazing adventures together.

There are so many other swimmers that I met all over the world, in my beloved Russia, who I never planned to visit and somehow the ice has introduced us and I fell in love with the Russian people. The colourful Irish people, North and Republic that received me with warmth and a great sense of humour, German, Austrian, Estonian, Scandinavian, Chinese, Australians, French, Americans (north and south) and last but not the least the British people, who embraced me and my passion with respect, wit and hospitality. You all showed me another side of humanity, a supporting and respectful one.

IISA and its people, board and swimmers, what an amazing bunch.

I also like to say a special thank you to Lisa Bell www.thewordarchitect.co.za , who advised me, structured my chaotic book and encouraged me to write this book.

And of course, the special person in my life, Sam, who gave me a new lease of life and showed me how the sun shines as she enters the room. Thank you.

Table of Contents

Foreword   11

Preface   13

Chapter 1   15
The Early Years – Kibbutz Life

Chapter 2   26
Rebel Rebel – The Teenage Years

Chapter 3   39
The Army

Chapter 4   65
The Fire

Chapter 5   73
Lesson in Survival

Chapter 6   82
The Student – University Years

Chapter 7   92
The Passion of Windsurfing

Chapter 8   97
Tokyo and Sushi

Chapter 9   112
Cadiz – A Bonfire of Vanities

Chapter 10   130

How I Met the Cold Sea

Chapter 11   139

Recovering from an Ice Swim

Chapter 12   146

Life with Celiac Disease

Chapter 13   151

Round Cape Peninsula Swim

Chapter 14   157

The Orange River 2000 km Challenge

Chapter 15   167

The Robben Island Night Swim

Chapter 16   175

Kinneret, The Sea of Galilee – and a Swim for Peace

Chapter 17   183

Antarctica I – Guinness World Record

Chapter 18   197

Lake Zurich Swim

Chapter 19   206

The Scariest Ice Swim of Them All – Tyumen Siberia

Chapter 20   217

The International Ice Swimming Association

Foreword

For over a decade, I have been in constant awe at Ram Barkai's physical feats, long-term vision, and leadership.

I have covered Ram's swimming challenges ever since he completed his first Ice Mile in 2009 in Lake Zurich. His solo swims around the world have set Ice Swimming standards for others to meet and exceed, but he has also played logistically demanding dual roles as the expedition leader and athlete in swims like the Patagonia Extreme Cold Water Challenge, the Antarctica Circle Challenge and the Ice Kilometre Swim, the 1st, 2nd, 3rd and 4th International Ice Swimming World Championships, Lesotho Ice Swimming and the Svalbard Ice Swimming Adventures deep inside the Arctic Circle by the North Pole.

Ram not only pushed himself to achieve unfathomable feats of ice swimming, but more importantly, he also established the International Ice Swimming Association to create a global framework and organization that allows thousands of adventurous souls to similarly push themselves physically, mentally, and emotionally. His talents and vision are the catalysts to the emerging sport of Ice Swimming. His charisma and boundless enthusiasm give inspiration and hope to others who wish to follow him in 'The Ice'.

In lakes, seas and rivers on five continents, from Antarctica to the Arctic Circle, his energy is always infectious, but he also always focuses on safety. He helps people believe in themselves in solo swims and competitions. In a sport with extreme physical demands held in extremely harsh and inhospitable environments, Ram has the unique ability to support and motivate successful people and those who face occasional failure and disappointment. It is one of the key pillars of his leadership style.

When, where, why, and how did Ram – a former financier who donned suits and ties in corporate boardrooms – discover and develop his ability to strip down to Speedos and willingly expose himself to such cold and pain – and motivate a generation of swimmers to follow him? *From Fire To Ice* tells his improbable journey from childhood to the establishment of the International Ice Swimming Association. His legacy and vision are set – but it is also still being formed and evolving.

Steven Munatones is a native of Southern California and the founder of the World Open Water Swimming Association (WOWSA), the Daily News of Open Water Swimming, the UltraMarathon Swim Series, and the Oceans Seven. He was awarded the Poseidon Award by the International Swimming Hall of Fame and has been honoured by the International Marathon Swimming Hall of Fame and USA Swimming. He served on the FINA Technical Open Water Swimming Committee, as a Technical Delegate for the Special Olympics World Summer Games, and as a commentator for the Olympic marathon swim at the 2008 Beijing Olympics. He has written over 20,000 articles on all disciplines of open water swimming since his first article in Swimming World Magazine in 1982.

Preface

It took me many years to cook this book in my mind, writing chapter after chapter and storing it deep inside my brain, below the ice sheet. I love telling stories and I love real stories, but I was never inspired to write a book. I am not sure how I ended up here, but many times when I told one of my colourful life and adventures stories, I was asked, "Why don't you write a book?" One day I set down and started writing. It's for my kids to keep and hopefully to laugh at times at their silly dad doing silly things and discovering life and inspire them to grow, explore with excitement no fear live their life to its fullest.

I always lived my life with my heart, trying not to forget my head in the process. It's a delicate balancing act. Too much heart gets you into trouble and too much head keeps you indoors. I was always in awe of others who knew at a young age exactly what they want to do in life, those who wanted to do something extraordinary with their lives at a young age. I always felt that I ended up doing extraordinary things in the spirit of the moment rather than with a precisely planned strategy. Writing this book gave me a look-back option to revisit my life journey, to look again at those many times when I had to choose right or left. One thing I have noticed was that I always chose the red pill *(The Matrix)* I have no doubt that I would grab the apple in the garden of Eden regardless of who gave it to me, knowledge and curiosity certainly played a huge part in my do or not do decisions.

Life was never meant to be easy for me. It may seem easy to others to see successes and results because they are visible while failures or struggles are many times hidden well and only available for the very few closest to me. I never look at choices as easy or hard, as short or long. I always judged options as the right ones regardless of the consequences. I could have certainly made my life easier had I managed to convince myself not to be so hard-headed and focused. Yet, it has proved me right many times and I knew that I am wired that way and trying to be someone I am not will backfire. My strength was my curse.

I was always drawn to philosophy rather than religion. My tests always showed a balanced brain, left and right, analytical and creative. This is why I never ended up being an artist or an accountant but a creative analyst. Philosophy has a great combo of both the right and left sides of the brain. I loved the zen I discovered through reading at a young age and during my years in the east. The zen of accepting outcomes without having them block the road ahead. I think it helped me a lot in my adventures and when I plunged myself into unknown and possibly life-threatening situations. I studied the possibilities, the outcomes, the pitfalls and now it was time to walk through it, no fear, staring it straight in the eyes, accepting the outcomes.

This book is just a tale of my journey through life. Everyone has a story to tell and everyone had interesting life has he or she chose to make it interesting. Interesting has a price like anything in life. I love to listen to people's real-life stories, not the sugar-coated, picture-perfect story. I love the real ones, the ones that make people get out of their comfort zone by choice or not and hearing them take life head-on with passion and a healthy sense of humour.

I tried to share the lessons learnt on my journey. Lessons from successes, many more failures and just experiences. I never liked to look back with regrets, I always like to look forward to the next experience and adventure but learning from my experiences and mistakes is invaluable.

I hope you'll enjoy this journey, laugh at my stories and maybe inspire you to not be scared to be yourself. In everything you do, be true to yourself and follow your dreams and passion because life goes in a flash and we must do our best to enjoy this journey.

Chapter 1
The Early Years – Kibbutz Life

It was around 2 a.m. and the adrenaline was pumping through my veins. My dad and I were running outside and he was holding my hand tightly.

We were making our way towards the bunkers and my little seven years old self was hugging my pillow to my chest while my dad carried my duvet. We heard a soft 'pheshew', the sound that the Katyusha rocket makes when it leaves its launcher and we heard the warning whistle that always followed. And then all was quiet. I knew that when the whistle stopped it meant the rocket was heading our way. My dad threw himself and me into the nearest bush on the side of the road. Maybe he did it out of protective instinct or to find some kind of shelter, but it would not have helped much had the rocket landed close. I remember the earth moving under our feet and thinking that the sound was so loud that it felt as if the rocket had landed on top of us.

But luckily, it fell a few hundred metres from us and we immediately got up and started running again. Within a few minutes, we had entered the bunker, which was full of kids and adults, excited and hyped up. I don't recall feeling fear, but I do remember the excitement, everyone shouting until one of the adults took control and ordered us all to go to sleep.

For us, it was normal. I grew up on a small kibbutz by the Sea of Galilee (Kinneret), 3 km from the Golan Heights and the border with Syria. We were 9 km from the Jordan border and 1 km away from a big army ammunition storage that the Syrian and Jordanians kept on targeting. Nights like that became routine and as things got busier, we started to go to sleep in the bunkers avoiding the midnight sprints. Again, this was normal for us, but looking back it was a completely surreal way of growing up. Life was completely normal during the day, well normal for a kibbutz lifestyle, but in the evening, we would all go to sleep in a shelter. Every now and then during the day, we would stand and watch Israeli fighter planes having a dogfight with a Syrian Mig above the Kinneret. We always won. Seeing fighter planes speeding low above the water to avoid Syrian radar and then rise into the Golan Heights for some mission was just a routine occurrence.

Before the 1967 war or the six days war where Israel took over the Golan Heights, the surrounding fields were lying under the eyes of the Syrian border posts. They used to snipe at tractors and people in the fields so most people who worked the fields by the border fence used armed tractors and had some military presence. Our kibbutz often suffered rocket attacks that would hit the dairy farm, the chicken farms or other areas. I can't recall how our parents managed this life but in a twisted way, I had a great childhood surrounded by nature, seas, fields and plenty of action.

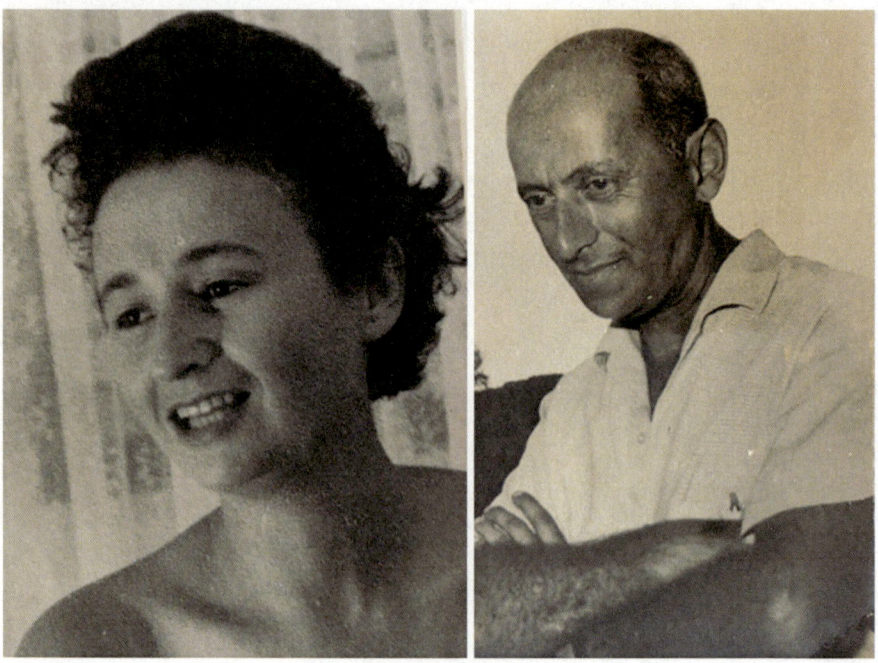

Mom   Dad

My parents grew up in Romania. My dad was born in Cluj, the capital of Transylvania and my mom grew up in Braila, a small town south of Bucharest. Transylvania, 'the place behind the forests', is the northern part of Romania

16

and it is separated from the rest of Romania by a large mountain range covered with pine trees. It borders with Hungary in the north and geographically it fits better with Hungary than Romania. Transylvania used to be part of the Austro-Hungarian Empire, so my father spoke Hungarian at home and Romanian at school. My dad died when I was 21 years old, still in the army and long before I managed to get to know him as an adult. He was a very talented hard man who was brought up in a very strict household. He did soften quite a bit before he passed away, but I always regret not having the chance to grow older with him. I was a true rebel without a cause as a child although not much has changed and I demanded independence from a young age.

The kibbutz was an idealistic form of social structure that was based on true Marxism and communism. It was based on such a strong ideology that it worked very well for quite some time. In the kibbutz, everyone was equal, well, mostly. Everyone who worked there was no exception. People worked where they were required, so most were found in the fields. Some worked in service-type industries, such as the dining room, laundry, kitchen and some assumed responsibility for the finances, the building and other areas that were essential to our existence. There were no luxuries or indulgences. You were there to do something useful. Your ambitions were not a desirable topic of discussion. We shared everything and when I say everything, I mean everything. At some stage, people were sharing each other's wives or husbands, not intentionally or openly, although that was not part of the ideology, it was a by-product of a small ideological society that shared a lot with no privacy.

As a child, I had no real personal possessions. I had very few toys at my parents' place, but we the kids went to a kindergarten where we could play with the toys. We saw our parents for only a few hours every day from around 4 pm to 8 pm when we went to bed. We would only sleep in our parents' house on Friday nights because the kindergartens closed on Saturday. Each kindergarten accommodated around three age groups and in our case around 15 kids. Our kibbutz was a relatively small one with around 300 people in total. Our everyday life revolved around the kindergarten, which was for all intense and purposes, our home. We ate in a big dining room where the entire kibbutz used to gather three times a day. The food was awesome and plentiful. The lifestyle was great and carefree with no crime and no worries other than the raids at night. Our regional school was a few kilometres away from where around 15 to 20 kibbutzim sent their kids.

The Barkai clan
Left: Rebel me, Hemi with his newborn son, Mom, Amos, Dad and Yair
in the front

My kibbutz was literally on the water of the Kinneret and my parents' house was in the first row of the beachfront. Needless to say, I spent most of my time at the beach or in the water. None of us owned our clothes. We shared it all, yes, even underpants. Twice a year in spring and autumn, we marched to the clothing warehouse in the kibbutz and were kitted out with enough clothes for the season. We got called in one by one and we felt like it was Christmas. We were given around six pairs of pants, a few shirts and underpants, socks and a jacket. Most of the clothes were handed down from older kids. We were like one huge family. There was no waste. Our clothes were all tailored in the kibbutz from the same material and we looked like an orphanage wearing the same shirt and pants. But we were so excited and proud as we didn't know anything else.

I think I was 13 years old when I was first given my very own personal pair of pants and a shirt. I marvelled that they were actually mine and that I could keep them forever or as long as they fit me. I recall getting a jersey from a visiting uncle from the city. It was way too big but also way too dear to just give it to the collective kibbutz, so we kept it in the cupboard for a few years until it fit me.

A little history on my family and the kibbutz. My father lost all of his family in the Holocaust. He left home when he was 18 years old never to see his parents, sister and other family members ever again. They were taken to Auschwitz and never returned.

The kibbutz was founded in 1941 by a group of immigrants mostly from Romania and Hungary. The first wave that founded the kibbutz, my parents' generation were mostly Holocaust survivors at various stages. Some had experienced it as kids and some as young adults. Many had their tattooed number on their arm, few were subjected to horrific medical experiments but many lost most of their families in the Holocaust. Again, this reality was just normal for us as kids. Everyone had a dark story, a huge burden and had survived some kind of horrific episode. The Holocaust was a very integral part of our lives as we had grown up with it, had heard the horror stories and were reminded of our history all the time.

I remember that as much as it touched us, it was a part of our life in Israel, we were safe and free of anti-Semitism experiences and it was hard for us to relate to it. It was only later as we grew up that we fathomed the reality of what had happened in the Second World War and we started to understand where our parents had come from.

My father had been very active in Europe with the Jewish efforts to help Jews to escape and reach Israel. He read and spoke around seven languages and was a very talented man although he never managed to go to university. He was as we called 'auto-deduct', a self-taught man and he seemed to be doing everything. His main job in the kibbutz was to manage all the building activities. He was involved in the design, landscaping, building and finance. Our kibbutz had 300 people and because of the many public places that needed assistance, he would often have dining room duty in the evening. He could be seen serving food or washing dishes. In addition, once a month he would have guard duty for a week during the night as well as several other responsibilities.

He was also a self-taught electrician and carpenter and I can remember clearly that every time there was a power failure, someone would knock on our door and call my dad to sort it out. He read mostly in English and French. I didn't understand why at the time, but I remember a little van from the French embassy would stop at our house once a month. It was the mobile library and my father exchanged books with them. I used to get all the Rin Tin Tin magazines in French but it never bothered me. I loved it. We had bookshelves full of science fiction novels in English that my dad devoured all the time.

With our mother in the kibbutz
Left: Hemi, me, Amos and my Mom. Yair hasn't arrived yet.

My father was the true authority in the house. While my mom was busy cooking or worrying about the rest of us, he developed an order amongst us. I was one of four brothers. Two were older than me and then there was our late edition. Four sons and a hard father was a tough place to be. When food was on the table, there was always a hierarchy in order and size. There wasn't much talking around the table but later on, when my dad got weaker and soften up a lot, it was much easier. My dad had a very dry sense of humour, accepted no complaints and had a 'get on with it' kind of attitude. It wasn't easy for us, especially for my oldest brother, Hemi, as well as for my second oldest brother, Amos. They got the brunt of his wrath many a time. I, fortunately, missed some of it as he got softer as he got older.

Mom and Dad

He had his first heart attack when I was close to 16 years old. I will never forget it because life changed completely after that. Up to that point, we all had to have our hair cut, very short, every two weeks. A cut meant no scissors, only a shaver and usually set on a number three up to number six. It was a five-minute job and we would all stand outside, waiting for our turn, like a conveyer belt. You must remember that this was the 60s, The Beatles era, where long hair was the in thing. And here we were forced to walk around like little soldiers with spiky hair.

The day my dad went to the hospital with his first heart attack, I stopped cutting my hair. When he came back from the hospital, he was a softer, more pliable person and strangely, he never asked me to cut my hair again. I didn't. I grew it all the way to when I was 18 years old and then had to have it all shaved off for the army. Before the army, I was a true Beatlemania boy! And no one was allowed to touch my hair.

The 1967 war was a surreal experience. All the men disappeared and we got rushed down to the bunkers for six solid days. Every now and then we were allowed to climb out and watch the war unfolding in front of our eyes. We watched the endless lines of tanks like ants climbing in a convoy up the mighty Golan Heights and taking over. The army was everywhere. We had a regiment of tanks parked in the kibbutz fringe and the roads were covered with an army of all kinds going and coming. I remember soldiers throwing packets of Syrian cigarettes at people on the side of the roads. Like the naughty eight-year-old boys we were, we managed to get our grubby hands on a few packets and tried smoking them. Needless to say, I found it quite disgusting and it put me off smoking, well at least until I turned 18.

Hemi, my oldest brother, had just joined the army and was taken straight into the war. For whatever reason, he was always the unlucky brother in the family. If there was a war, he found himself in the middle of it. North or south, he was there for the 1967 war, the 1973 war, the Attrition war and the Lebanon war. He was an officer in the tanks and he ended up in some very uncomfortable situations. I remember a few stories of him being stuck in the middle of the battlefield with a broken cannon and unable to reverse. His team placed the cannon in the air as if they were hit and then they just sat there in the middle of the crazy war frenzy waiting for evacuation. They were completely exposed and were hoping that they would somehow go unnoticed and survive. Thankfully, they did.

For a reason still unclear to me, I started to develop a very strong personality and a sense of independence. That hasn't left me to date and although it helped me tremendously to achieve many things, it also made my life very difficult. I developed a strong sense of what was right and wrong and I didn't hold my tongue in expressing my strong uncompromising opinions about it. Although I was correct many times, the way I went about informing others turned my teenage years into a very interesting period. My sense of right and wrong wasn't linked to conventional social rules or norms. Right and wrong were not a vague flexible open for interpretation issue, for me it was quite a clear issue you honour regardless of consequences and when you made mistakes you own it and their consequences. I'm still working on softening that part, although grey areas never attracted me.

A clear memory I have, when I was about 11 years old, was when they started to build a holiday campsite next to the kibbutz. They had a shop, a restaurant and a few other facilities. For me, growing up in the kibbutz where no one carried money or used the money to purchase anything, was a huge development. We never had fizzy drinks growing up and it was a big luxury for us. We would make a plan at least once a month when we were lucky enough to go to the nearest city for an outing.

The campsite had a storage place full of Coke and Fanta bottles and it didn't take us long before we figured out a way to get in there and take a few bottles. I was the main instigator and arranged a few kids. We had a system and basically, we would each take a few bottles, hide them underneath our shirts and run to the nearby sea. There, we had a corner ready with strings and stones. We used to tie each bottle to a five-metre string, attach it to a heavy stone and fling the bottle into the water. That was our hiding place and our fridge. In our minds, because it was 40°C outside, we simply couldn't drink a hot fizzy drink. We would go back in the evenings, fish out the bottles and sit on the beach with a bonfire drinking our chilled Coke or Fanta. We felt like Gods! It was such an adventure, such a treat and loads of fun. We justified our actions by telling ourselves that we were just taking the bottles from our kibbutz, which our parents owned. That reasoning was good enough for us.

Like anything else, more kids found out and we needed more bottles. One day as we were walking pregnant with seven to eight bottles each, we were confronted by one of the adults. It was a short chase and a painful hearing with a few of the kibbutz leadership. The fun was over and I was identified as the ringleader. That was the beginning of my bad reputation in the kibbutz. We did plenty of other naughty things that, in those days in the Kibbutz, were considered almost criminal, but we had some fun and we were naughty; stealing ice creams from the dining room storage, smuggling watermelons to the beach for a party and many other minor adventures. I was fearless for whatever reason and I enjoyed it. Again, I saw the taking of food and drink as if I were walking into my parents' kitchen, aka the kibbutz dining room. We didn't have much at home and although we never had to worry about food, we didn't grow up with indulgences. These little treats were our escapisms.

A little on my time at social work after school…

I was 17 years old, a high school dropout and I still had my teacher's parting words echoing in my ears, 'Some people are born to work in the fields, nothing to be ashamed about it.' Today, she is long gone, cancer at 70 years of age, so I heard, yet I still can't forget those words. She was 25y at the time and she summed up my life potential in a few words. Well, thankfully, life turned out to be quite different.

I was back in the fields working and pondering about the time left before I got called to the army. Some people took a gap year doing some guided social work at remote locations in Israel; small towns that had little government support but were critical as a strategic foot on the ground by the borders. These towns had a lot of domestic social issues; drunken parents, prostitution, drugs and street gangs. My brother, Amos, did a year there before the army, so I thought it would be a better experience and a different one. I ended up in the same residence as my brother and in the same room. I was based in Kiryat Shemona and this was in 1975.

The work entailed tutoring a ten-year-old kid that couldn't read and write due to domestic issues. He was a nice and keen child, but I was far too young to understand the weight of the social issues surrounding him and the others in the community. We were there to help, but any sign of patronising or 'we are here to help' raised anger and resentment among the locals. They knew exactly the reality they were growing up in and they knew how privileged we were, maybe not financially but socially. It was a very fine line we were treading on and took a lot to not piss off the street gangs who used to pay us regular, not so friendly, visits and remind us that they controlled the streets. As long as that was clear, we were welcome to stay.

Living in a commune with nine others, aged 17 and 18, was quite fun. We had lots of freedom and we looked after ourselves. We had a living expenses budget and we took our responsibilities very seriously. Regular support was received from professional physiologists since we were untrained and certainly out of our depth. As time went by, we got too tangled and confused about our huge responsibilities. We ended up divided into two groups, which were 'the deep thinkers and 'the fun-loving'. I ended up somewhere in between. I did take my responsibilities seriously, but I was only 17 years old and I knew that it was way above my head and besides I was soon to be off to the army. Fun was certainly a very important ingredient at that time in my life.

That balance between responsibility and fun is something that I kept as a common thread all through my life. Later on, I got used to being told, "I can't really figure you out, Ram...Seriously? Fun?" I have always endeavoured to keep my word and deliver the goods 100%, but I always did it in my way and had to see the funny side of everything. Sarcasm and wit had become my strongest attribute, some liked it, many didn't really get it and some hated it. I suppose that's why I love Oscar Wilde's stories, that subtle wit and in some ways, that no fear of criticism attitude.

We ended up getting more physiological support and advice as a group than we actually gave our students. It got seriously heavy quickly. That was the first time in my life that I met 'the group dynamic sessions'. As you can imagine, being 17, I hated it. I remember leaving a session feeling like nine people had just thrown up on me and I was supposed to say 'thank you for sharing that with me. I also realised that as much as everyone desperately asked for honest feedback, most of them couldn't handle it and their defence mechanism turned against you. I started to learn to refine my honesty and endeavour to keep it constructive. To date, it is still a work in progress.

Being a couple of kilometres from the Lebanese border brought back many memories from home. An occasional siren, the soft sound of the rocket exiting, that 'pheshew'... and the wait to hear it crashing somewhere nearby. It always felt like it was landing next door. But these rockets, *'katyusha'*, were not very effective and they could literally land through a roof in the next room, destroy it but you would be fine, partially deaf and in need of clean trousers maybe but fine.

Chapter 2
Rebel Rebel – The Teenage Years

Me, as a cheeky teenager

As I grew up and started developing an interest in the fairer gender, I had to face the reality of no easy commute options.

Our parents didn't own cars and in fact, my parents never learnt to drive a car in their life until their very last day. We had bicycles as our main transportation and tractors to work in the fields.

Riding a bicycle through the dark fields at night with my best mate, Itai, to visit girls in another kibbutz was dangerous, scary but mostly uncool. Tractors were the main means of cool transportation, but one required a licence, which only arrived after turning 16 years of age. So, stealing a tractor to visit a friend or a girl was mission impossible. Not all of them had lights and most were locked to prevent us from taking them and of course possibly causing some damage that would make it unusable to work the fields the next day. Needless to say, none of this stopped me and a few of us naughty kids from traversing the fields late at night for a party in another kibbutz or hoping to be noticed by some pretty girl from class. We were all so naive those days. There was no alcohol, drugs or crime. It was just naughty fun. But I was building a reputation of being a real fearless rebel.

When I moved to high school, my mind was elsewhere, not girls though, just life. I read a lot, questioned much and I disagreed too many times. The kibbutz social system was getting to me. I started to see the other side of this ideological Pleasantville. I started to see how some abused the system and how some manipulated the system. My father was as straight as an arrow and that caused him a lot of grief. He was uncompromising about our ideology and our purpose, but we had second, third and more waves of people joining the kibbutz with different background cultures and ideologies and that killed my dad. He had sacrificed his whole life for that ideology. Because of his background, he had very powerful and influential friends that tried to take him away from the land and cajoled him to move to the city, and assume a bigger role in Israel, but he was committed and unmovable. He seemed to see it as if it was something he owed his lost family. I respected him and still do for his tenacity and perseverance.

The older I grew, the more I started challenging many things around me and especially authority, a habit that caused me a lot of trouble in my life and especially later on in the army. High school seemed like a waste of time for me. Some of the subjects were very interesting like maths, physics and Hebrew, but the rest annoyed me. I struggled with Bible studies in particular. While I had read the book a couple of times and found it fascinating, I couldn't stand unpacking it repeatedly. For me, it was a great story that had some reflection on our history but I was much more interested in the future. I read a lot; literature, poetry, science fiction and many other genres. I grew up with classical music at home and lots of it. I loved music and spent hours and hours listening to music whenever I could. I loved the sea too and you would find me in the water every opportunity I got, but mostly sailing the Kibbutz's dingy.

It wasn't long before I started to miss classes. It wasn't such a big deal for me and I had no problem keeping up with the subject matter, but I was just bored to tears. Normal life had my attention. All the teachers were from the surrounding kibbutzim, some were very young and simply bad teachers, in my opinion at least, but some were just priceless and I loved every class with them. It was around that time that I started to develop a deep sense of respect for intelligence, intellect and competence. I struggled with teachers that were plain and average but tried to behave like the masters of the universe. I simply struggled to pay the required respect to them.

Within the first month at my high school, I got into trouble. I always sat in the back of the class by the window, mostly because I liked the view and the fresh air, but in truth, because I wanted to be left alone, unnoticed. My reasoning was that if I wanted to be noticed, I had my ways. It was biology class and I was rocking on my chair against the wall, watching the class in front of me. Kids were shouting answers to questions all over the place and it was chaos. The teacher shouted back for quiet and made it clear, "You will only be noticed if you raise your hand and get permission to talk."

A few minutes later, he asked the class a question and knowing the answer I raised my hand. The teacher picked the pupils one by one and they all got the wrong answer. I knew that I knew the right answer, but I wasn't noticed, despite waving my hand desperately in the back row. Other pupils raised their hands, got noticed and some even shouted out the answer. Suddenly, I felt that I had had enough and I shouted out the teacher's name trying to get his attention. My voice could carry quite powerfully if I chose it to and the entire class went quiet, looking from me to the teacher.

I was unfazed. It was my turn and I knew I had the answer. It was my time now was what I thought. But the teacher thought otherwise. I was told to leave the class immediately and I refused. I stated my case, but he wasn't listening. He wanted me out because I presented him with an opportunity to demonstrate his authority. Well, he had picked the wrong guy for this. I simply refused to leave the class. As far as I was concerned, I had done nothing wrong and I kept on defending my action.

Finally, the teacher said, "Either you leave the class or I do!" Well, that was an easy one for me because I wasn't going anywhere. I had done nothing wrong. The teacher stormed out and left the class followed by a thunder of silence. I never cared about being a popular guy in the school or a hero and I didn't do it to score any points. This had been between me and the teacher and he was clearly in the wrong. I found out later that that was the first time it had ever happened in the school history and of course, I was sent home for a week for the first time and certainly not the last. Luckily, my dad, who was bald by that stage, couldn't go grey over this indiscretion.

My home kibbutz by the Kinneret lake
Just below the Golan Heights

High school turned out to be an adventure actually. I was interested in everything but my studies. The reality of growing up in a kibbutz in those days certainly influenced my behaviour and perception of life. In the kibbutz, all you had to do was to follow the norms, work and fit in then your future was secure. As you grew older, you could move to better and bigger units. After the army, you got your own house, small but functional and suitable, a furnishing allowance, a monthly allowance, free food and use of all the kibbutz facilities. When and if you got married, you got a better and bigger unit and so it went on. There was always work that required hands and if you wished to take on more responsibility, it was up to you. You might have even managed to get in the queue for a higher education one day and be able to go to university or higher studies but only if your subject was useful to the kibbutz.

Many things have changed since then and most kibbutzim have evolved with various industries, freedom of study and subjects, kids being allowed to live with their parents and many also have privatised to some form of collective, private ownership structure. But in those days, your future was paved out for you until your last day. If you wondered where you would end up, all you had to do was cross the main road and visit the kibbutz cemetery tucked between grapefruit orchids and a banana field. Everyone had a designated spot. My father lies next to my mother. Life was great and simple, no worries, no need to panic about education, employment, housing and the future.

What it did do, however, was allow for more and more mediocrity to settle in comfortably. Leaving the kibbutz was as bad as defecting and betraying your family. Sons who left used to come back sometimes and visit, trying not to be seen, finding a quiet time to get to their parents' home and settle in there. Some dared to come to the main dining room on Friday evenings with their parents, a spouse and sometimes their children. We used to call them weekend guests because many of them had just started life outside the kibbutz having no support structure out there, no money and no tools to deal with the big wide world.

Many times, they came to visit as a relief and went back to the city with their parents, quietly and secretly loading the back of their little car with vegetables, fruits and other food products we had. They needed all the help they could and the system simply wouldn't allow their desperate parents to assist them. It took me a few years to see the paradox in our 'perfect' system where parents who had sacrificed everything, they had to build this ideal life couldn't afford to help their kids in any way. It was the perfect golden cage. As long as you were in, you were 100% looked after, but if you chose to walk out, you could take nothing with you and get nothing from them.

My parents didn't have a system to save money because they received no salary or any other income. They had no assets or savings. They basically had very little to nothing, but everything they needed was provided for free. This carefree life led to many youngsters not matriculating going straight to the army and back to the kibbutz life or work. They would get married, reproduce and so on.

For some, it was an ideal life, but for me, it started to become a nightmare. I felt as if I was in some form of a cage and my future was out of my hands. My future was being discussed and decided by others without even consulting with me. Maybe it wasn't so bad, but it clashed head-on with my personality. I needed freedom, lots of it. I didn't like being told what to do and how to do it. Having said that, I loved my teenage days there. I worked in the fields very hard. I loved the fields, the outdoors, the animals and the simple healthy life. If

I wasn't in the field, I was by the sea. We had a few small sailing boats, a speedboat, horses and loads of freedom.

But I digress. High school started to become a real nuisance. I knew I certainly wasn't dumb but I was essentially bored. My grades were either A or D or F, nothing in between.

Dressed as a Roman citizen with Itai on Purim

I developed a strong sense of pride and refused to copy or cheat. I also refused to study subjects that I hated. I remember exam sittings where I simply had no idea what to write because I hadn't studied that subject. I would stare at the paper for a few minutes and then walk out of the class. Needless to say, a big red F would follow. I knew I had to pass so with some subjects I didn't like, I would somehow manage to get just above the pass rate.

I didn't look for trouble nor caused trouble, but the trouble did find me. At a point, I had missed too many classes and eventually got kicked out for not listening, reading my own books or playing games with my mate next to me. My lack of interest certainly irritated many of my teachers who would find ways to pick on me, single me out or stand me up in order to embarrass me in front of everyone.

At 16 years old, as part of my rebellious lifestyle and growing my hair, I decided to stop wearing shoes. I spent over a year walking around barefoot, summer, winter, city or on the kibbutz. I still can't believe that it had been tolerated, but I got away with this. I think my dedication to work at the kibbutz let me off the hook many times.

I loved working at the dairy farm. It became a passion and somewhat an obsession. My brothers worked there as well, so I joined them sometimes and learnt the skills. Milking cows, the machinery, delivering calves, treating sick cows and running away from the young bulls were all part of my growing up.

In 1973, I was in grade ten and a real young rebel, the dedicated longhaired Beatle fan. But then the war erupted again. I remember the day it started very clearly. It was Yom Kippur, the most sacred day in the Jewish religion and the whole country came to a halt. Most were fasting for 24 hours and spending the day in Shul, as was the normal process over this time. My family, while a very liberal and intellectual home, didn't follow religion as the others did. We respected it but didn't follow it. That's just the way it was.

It was around 2 pm and all the young guns were down at the football field watching a local match. For us, it was just another holiday. But it all happened very quickly. Aeroplanes started to buzz above our heads, and busses arrived and started picking up the young men to take them off to the army gathering locations. Radios were turned on and we were all sat to listen to codes being repeated on the airwaves.

Each reservist in the army had his own unit code for emergency and when it was called out on the radio, you had to go pack your stuff and wait by the kibbutz gate for the bus to take you to the front. Within a few hours, the kibbutz was emptied of all the young men who were 18 years and older. There was a maximum age limit but I'm not sure what that was. We heard that the Syrian army had taken over the Golan Heights and was heading our way. Talks of evacuation could be heard all around me. Both my elder brothers were in the army at the time. Hemi was a reservist officer in tanks and Amos was in special forces, an ex-Seal. Both were taken to fight that day.

That war was much longer than the previous one I had experienced and had a very different feel to it. Israel was under serious threat of survival. We heard horror stories about what they predicted that war would reveal and possible defeat was, for the first time, considered.

The first two days, while Israel reorganised itself from a deep religious coma into a full-blown war, were scary. The young soldiers were literally acting as cannon shields waiting for the reserve army to assemble and join the war. After two or three days, as the army started to get the reserves back up to join the front, the balance of power changed and Israel started to gain control of the fronts. Both my brothers spent the next few months fighting in the south and the north. Many years later, I heard their war stories and the miracle of their survival.

In the kibbutz, I suddenly found myself an adult with huge responsibilities. The men had just disappeared but the fields and the animals still needed care. A domestic cow needs to be milked three times a day consistently or it will get sick from generating too much milk that remains in its udder. We had work to do, a lot of it and no time to think about it. In a crazy turn of events, we were all running the farm. The school was shut down for six months and the focus was on survival and following up on the men fighting somewhere but not far away at all. The war was all around us; the roads were packed with the army in all forms but mostly tanks moving up and down the Golan Heights and the Syrian front. There were convoys making their way down, licking their wounds and resting while fresh ones streamed up into the front.

Israeli tanks

We spent our time working around 15 to 16 hours a day and then rushing to the centre where all the army was gathering just outside our kibbutz. With a tractor and a trailer loaded with big pots of hot tea, some food and anything we could get to give the soldiers, we did all we could to alleviate their suffering. I remember trying to get some information from the tanks and infantry soldiers about my brothers. It was chaos but it was amazing to see and be part of. It is a strange human behaviour. There is nothing like a war that threatens one's life to bring everyone together, selflessly giving anything they can to help. A soldier was a hero and everyone would shower them with love and help. We worked days and nights and I was basically running the kibbutz dairy farm, finding myself dealing with huge issues and making decisions that were way beyond what anyone prepared me for. But it was also amazing. I managed and it all worked out in the end. No one complained. No one hesitated. We were all very focused and just got on with it.

News started to come in that the war had turned and we had managed to reclaim taken territories. Our armies were going deeper into Syria and Egypt. But war has its price. Names started to come in too, dead or missing in action and horror war stories from all fronts. This was very unlike the six days war. There were no celebrations and songs of heroism. It was a bloody war that took many lives and shattered us to the bones. We were young adults and all we wanted to do was to join our forces and fight with them.

My father was the kibbutz secretary at the time, a huge responsibility in times of war. He was doing his duty night and day relentlessly. At the time, of course, none of us imagined he had only a few years left in him. I sometimes wonder if it hadn't been for that war if he may have stayed a little while longer with us on this earth.

When the war was over, the school reopened and life started to get back to normal. The majority of the men came back from the war, and some rotated back to service every few months but life had to go back to normal. The school was so remotely uninteresting and at that stage, I decided I no longer want to continue announcing my retirement from intellectual life. I told my family that I wished to dedicate my life to the fields and my beloved cows. I wasn't the only one. The war must have had a huge effect on our generation in many aspects. I just couldn't fathom the relevance of studying in high school when the world had nearly gone down before my very eyes. I spent the rest of my grade ten working and enjoying the study-free life. I felt like a young adult and I couldn't go back to being a child again and being told what to do every day.

The summer holiday finally arrived and I realised that maybe I had made a mistake as I was missing my friends from school. I wasn't an adult yet and I couldn't have a social life with the kibbutz adults, so as much fun and rewarding as it was, I decided to go back to school and attempt to finish it. I got on my bicycle and travelled to another kibbutz to meet my teacher whom I made extremely happy with my decision to retire from school. I got to her house, nervously knocked on the door and there she was, already with a stern disapproving look on her face. She probably had hoped I would disappear from her life completely. I explained my wish to return to school and interestingly enough, she said yes. However, since I had missed all the final exams, I would have only a few weeks to study and prepare for those exams. Needless to say, I had actually missed the entire year. Her condition for me to return was that I pass all the exams else I was not welcome back. Nothing like a good challenge for Rebel Ram. So, I spent the last few weeks of the holiday cramming none stop and writing all the exams in a few days and managed to pass them all to my teacher's grave disappointment.

The WWII memorial outside my home in the Kibbutz

I went back to school, grade 11, my final year before matric. I honestly think I tried my best and kept to myself mostly trying hard not to tell the teachers what I thought if I didn't agree with their methods or subject. Math and physics were great and acted as a sanity place for me.

I forgot to mention that living in the kibbutz you start working in the fields when you are young.

As a primary school scholar, you spend a few hours a week in the fields, but as a high school student, one day a week is a working day. You wake up at sunrise, work a full day just as an adult would do and go back to school the next day. It was normal for us and I believe it taught us the responsibility of a young adult from a young age.

Life was good but we were not spoiled, at all. At school, in grade 11, we had a half-day choice every Wednesday; either to go to the valley garage and stare at tractors while someone explained to us exactly how they worked or to join the girls for a cooking class in an air-conditioned room, eating the food together when you were done. For me, it was a no-brainer! I didn't care about my image or tractors. I had tractors in my life all the time and spending the afternoon with the girls, cooking and eating sounded just perfect. I was the only male in the class but it didn't take long for half of the boys to weigh up the options, swallow their macho pride and join us in cooking and having fun.

One day in the middle of the cooking class, about two months into the first term, my teacher walked in and asked me to join her. I had no idea what was coming. I wasn't a perfect pupil; I knew trouble always found me but I didn't expect that. I was told to sit down in a room and was given a lecture about life and purpose, about my future and destiny. Then she dropped the proverbial bomb on me. She said, "Ram, some people belong to the working class. Look at your parents and your friend's parents. There is nothing to be ashamed of. I believe that this is your future." I sat there with my mouth open, not believing that my teacher actually believed in what she was saying.

My father could have easily ended up with a PhD in some science or other, in a highly responsible position serving our country. My mother was also very intelligent and educated, but she followed my dad at the age of 18 to never see her parents again, choosing to work on the farm all her life. My parents chose that life, following their ideology and leaving behind everything they ever had. Now here was this teacher deciding that my future was in ploughing the land with my hands until I died. I had never felt that working the fields or the cows was beneath me or the domain of the uneducated simple people. I did accept that it was my life and I loved it, but I also knew that I was restless and that I would eventually find another path in life. I didn't respond or beg and cry for a second chance. I simply walked out and went home. I left my school bag, my books and everything I had on my desk never to see it again.

It was time.

I saw that teacher again, only once, before I went to university never to see her again after that. I only found out a few years ago that at a class reunion, a few past students approached her. She was old and sick by that stage but, apparently, these few, then quite successful and with family, went to her to remind her of what a terrible teacher she had been and that they would never forget that. She had been shocked and completely unaware of how her behaviour had affected them.

I learnt from a very young age about the abuse of power and have met it many times in my life following school. I have learnt to loathe it and the people who think they can wield their egotistical wand whenever they want. I will never forget how much such a relatively irrelevant person in your life can affect your life so negatively. I don't know how it affected me, maybe it made me stronger and more stubborn, but the fact that I never forgot it means that it most definitely affected me deeply somehow.

Many years later, when one of my daughters experienced some turbulence in her early high school career, I met with all her teachers. She was bunking too many classes and was causing a lot of problems in her classes. Sounds familiar? She was also a marked child; stereotyped and potential for expulsion. I asked her mother, my ex-wife, to gather a meeting with all the teachers in her school. As it was, with my hectic work, I arrived 30 minutes late, which was extremely rude and embarrassing. My ex-wife was sitting there alone with 13 teachers trying to soften the surface for my arrival, which she knew was not going to be smooth, to say the least. I apologised for my late arrival and listened carefully to something I had heard a long time ago. "Your daughter doesn't fit in. She is causing a lot of problems for her peaceful environment."

I must admit, the teachers and the headmaster were very polite and by no way as arrogant and assuming as my teacher had been, but the song was the same. I probably could have expressed myself better at that moment, however, I certainly got the message across. "Being different is not wrong. You should find a way to deal with it and nurture it. She is a bright and wonderful child. Don't do to her what has been done to me before." My daughter ended up with straight As in matric and she is now studying for her masters in astrophysics. She certainly will have plenty of mountains to climb, but I am proud of her and of all my children who are not scared to be who they are and follow their passion regardless of how difficult it can be in our society.

Back to the kibbutz. I had become an official member of the working class or the labour party, as it was called in the kibbutz. I had seven months before my army life would begin and I was tired of the fields. I had seen too many cow's udders that would last me for the rest of my life. I needed a change. So, I decided to join a voluntary group as a young social worker in a small town on the border of Lebanon. It was fun and interesting and I learnt a great deal. We had to work with some street gangs and kids from broken homes. Even though I was very young, it gave me a great perspective on other life forms in Israel. Aside from the fact that every few weeks we had to dive under our beds or kitchen tables when rockets hit the city, it was great. I can't say I ever got used to rockets hitting the city in the middle of the night. I guess I just learnt to deal with it but never liked it.

Chapter 3
The Army

Basic training tanks
Dust, dust and dust

In Israel, everyone has to go to the army. It may have relaxed a little nowadays, but when my time came, there was no question of going. And coming from a kibbutz, we really had no choice.

Army meant active service in a combat unit. The kibbutzim in Israel have changed a lot in the past 40 years. Back in those days, we were very proud of being part of a kibbutz. We were considered the elite of the country. I can only think that it was viewed that way because of the people who formed the kibbutzim. They were pioneering the elite front of idolatry. So, we did what was asked of us selflessly. That changed eventually, as these things do, much to my father's dismay. By the time I was of age, only 3% of the population were living in a kibbutz while around 30% of all officers in the army were from a kibbutz.

But then it was my turn…

Nothing can prepare you for the army. Back in my day, we had no social media and very little TV or relevant movies. In Israel, at the time, everyone had to go to the army, unless their physical or psychological profile was very low, which ended up being a double-edged sword. With a very low profile, you would have struggled to find a job those days. However, the army always found some use for you regardless of your background or education. This introduced a very interesting element to the service by creating this massive melting pot of all walks of life in Israeli society.

For me, it was the first time in my life that I got exposed to the world outside our kibbutz. Of course, I had been outside and met other parts of society, but I was always protected and shielded from the 'outside' and it was always for short periods. This time, there was nowhere to run to. It was a huge eye-opener, a scary one.

Suicide and depression were more common in the Israeli army than in other armies. Sure, there were armies where conscription was voluntary but the army itself was less hectic. However, for me, it was just normal. Many years later, travelling around the world, I realised how 'unnormal' it really was, especially to be forced to join the army at the tender age of 18 years.

From the age of around 17, the army starts to scout for new 'fresh meat' as we used to call it. We used to receive mail and visits to the school from the army telling us about the various options, such as the navy, air force and special forces. Where I grew up and during the time I grew up, there were no questions about choice. It had to be a combat unit of some form; air, sea or land, the way we were brought up in the kibbutz. Growing up by the Golan Heights, 3 km from Jordan and Syria, wars at your doorstep and being shelled often were common phenomenon, so it wasn't a hard sell.

In the army

Then it was time and we caught a bus to the army recruitment camp. I had long hair then, just about covering my shoulders as I was a real Beatnik rebel. But there I was entering this massive machine called the army. My classmate and I joined together and we stood in the queue receiving sequential numbers, which is a number that stays with you for the rest of your life. It tells others what year you joined the army and if you had to wake me up at 4 am and ask me for it, still, I could recite it to you without an issue.

We went through the fresh meat parade, a scary and humiliating process that turns you from a young, curious rebel into a khaki-suited number. I lost my hair and got kitted with clothing, shoes and a bed in one of the tents. I was quite relieved when the process was over. I no longer stood out in this khaki sea of numbers; I could quietly disappear into this sea. For whatever reason, I really wanted to join the navy seals where my brother, Amos, was once and I felt I knew quite a bit about the water. I was very comfortable in the water, but unfortunately, I was very underweight and quite a sickly child. At 1.79 cm, weighing in at 56 kg, nothing prepared me for what was coming. Fortunately, my profile was very good for the Army intelligence unit and I was approached and seduced about joining, but I was adamant I needed to do it the hard way.

Years later, I found out that 80% of the hi-tech start-ups are from the Israeli intelligence units. I suppose it is not the first time in my life that an easier opportunity presented itself and I just fell for the hard one, the more challenging one.

I spent a week in the navy seal camp and realised that there was a lot of running going on. Nights and days with heavy loads on that thin structure were hell. I had never liked running, but I did end up doing a lot of it in the army. I decided the seals were not my game and went back to base camp. My other brother, Hemi, was in tanks and I asked his advice. He was very honest saying, "It's a shit hole place to be in for three years, so go and become an officer as soon as you can. That is when it gets interesting and you have more control over your future and doings." My navy seal brother, Amos, was already over the novelty factor of seals and he was supportive as he thought life in The Seals was crazy and unhealthy. He was right. Many things have changed since, but the army was a very unhealthy place to be in, in those days. No sleep, bad nutrition, unsuitable gear and very little understanding of the damage they were inflicting on us.

Me the tank commander

Things already started to change when I left the army. They enforced six hours minimum sleep before live ammunition exercises, gear needed to be better fitted for the physical activity and the food improved drastically.

So, tanks it was. My roommate, Eldad, that joined up with me ended up in artillery. Later on, when we were both officers, his unit got caught in an ambush during a recce in Lebanon. He lost one eye, a big part of the other eye and endured many other injuries. He was lucky to come through it alive and today he lectures in cinematography, which was after he completed his PhD in Amsterdam.

I didn't see tanks for quite some time. First was basic training. It is around six months of taking you, breaking you physically and mentally and remoulding you back into the system. We ended up somewhere in the Gaza

Strip sands. The army never managed to break my spirit, however, and I did acquire a lot of respect for the other army veterans from around the world. We were kids, dressed up in uniform playing army. We had guns and live ammunition and we had no idea what was really going on. Many times, too tired to think or listen, we would just do! We were too young to understand wrong from right, as it wasn't our role. We were trained to become killing machines for when the time would come. It was as simple as that. This conflict of obeying an order and completing a mission versus the reality of what we were doing only came to challenge me years later.

But I digress. It was now reprogramming-Ram time. In the army, you are addressed by your surname and for whatever reason, just like in high school, I always got into trouble. The young corporals, who had sadistic joy in torturing us in basic training and possibly an IQ of river pebble, sensed my rebel tendencies. I kept quiet and did what I was told, but I didn't show fear and always saw the cynical side of our training. "Barkai, take that smirk off your face. Can you see that hill out there? The tree on top? Go and circle it in 30 seconds." Everything was done in 30 seconds, even two hours of punishment. Basic training was a haze of six months. We went home every two to three weeks for a short weekend, leaving on Friday morning and returning the Saturday evening. We slept an average of two hours a night, going to bed between 12 am and 2 am to be woken again between 4 am and 6 am, many times, sleeping in our clothes inside the sleeping bag. We also had two hours of guard duty every night and we were always dirty, tired and hungry.

We used to have some theoretical lessons but we couldn't stay awake for them, so to counter this, we all took up smoking, the best way to stay awake. I decided to smoke a pipe. It was different and it came with a few toys, which kept me busy without getting me into trouble. During lessons, I cleaned it, lit it, smoked it and played Sherlock Holmes. At night, during guard duty, which was guarding the ammunition storage and the camps, we were more petrified that we would be caught sleeping by the sergeant and end up in jail than any possible terrorist attacks. My pipe was an ideal company as it kept me awake and no one could see the little red dot of a cigarette end.

We learnt to respect the guns and that is one thing I kept from the army and have taught forward to others. We were told to treat our guns like our girlfriend. Never leave her alone. I am not sure if my girl at the time would be so happy to join me in the long-drop chemical toilets, but aside from that, the gun never left our arms. Losing your gun was probably the scariest thing that could happen to you. You would be thrown into jail for a few good months and I don't believe one ever recovered from that. The army created a culture of respect toward guns in Israel, where all the soldiers would carry a gun when they would go on leave. You never left your gun back at the army camp. If I went to the movies or a concert, a restaurant, a club or even a party, my gun would be around my shoulder with a magazine attached full of bullets. It was just the norm, men and women alike.

So, after six months, basic training was over and we were assigned to a tank's skills course for three months, not far from Tel Aviv, the big city. It was like moving to heaven. We had beds and floors rather than tents, mud and dust. We spent most of the time learning rather than being spun around hills and trees randomly like an electron in its atom sphere. It was getting interesting.

The tanks have three positions. Driver, which is terrible as you are basically locked up in a 76-ton vehicle, with a tiny hatched door above you, that weighs around 50kg, in a very small space. And most of the time, the canon is just above your hobbit space, so you are quite stuck. You can't see anything because of the dust and you mainly rely on intercom communication. Nevertheless, driving a 76-ton machine over basically everything can be fun sometimes. I still miss it and sometimes I drive my car as if it was my tank. The second position was the canon. You also got stuck inside, glued to the periscope, feeling your commander's knees on your spine. However, you get to aim and pull a trigger. The third was the loader, my position. It had its own cell with its own door and more space. You also could stand and stick your head out to see what was going on, as well as get some fresh air and have a chat with the commander. He had to rely on you for help sometimes because you were the only one who had eyes. The rest were practically blind with a small periscope and radio.

After three months, we were sent to the Golan Heights. We were all assigned a tank and a team and we started learning how to actually make it work. Although we weren't yet qualified for combat, we were on the border and we knew we could use our skills in case things got exciting. The course was over three months and was 30 minutes away from home. The Golan Heights was a beautiful, raw place and I started to develop my love for it. All in all, I spent around three years in the Golan Heights and by the end, I knew it like the back of my hand.

The Golan was taken by Israel in the 1967 war, so it was dotted with tiny old Arab villages riddled with bullets. Every intersection had a bloody heroic story from the 1948, 1956, 1967 and 1973 wars. There were a lot of bullet-riddled rusty vehicles on the sides of the roads, as well as many graves and memorial places too. It was real. We knew where we were and why we were there. The tank became our home. We learnt to sleep, eat, cook and smoke inside the tank. Some of this could have got us into trouble, but when you are stuck in a tank for a few days, you just adapt. You light a small gas burner in the middle of the 72 live shells, hand grenades and flammable oil or petrol and you boil some coffee, light a cigarette and chill.

When we didn't have cooked food, we used to receive canned food. To heat it, we used to lift the massive engine cover and leave it there for 20 minutes. Many times, we forgot about it or suddenly had to move and there would be a massive explosion with bully beef, diced carrots or corn flying all over the back of the tank. Cans do explode nicely if you leave them vacuum-sealed in the heat.

This course was hard, again, spending most of the time in the field in tough conditions, but it was starting to get interesting. We learnt some skills and formed some bonds with the team and the commander.

At the end of the three months, some of us were sent to tank commander's course and some to border duty. I did well and was selected to do the former. This took me to the other side of Israel, deep in the Sinai Desert. I ended up spending around 18 months in the desert and grew to love its raw and silent nature. Tanks move a lot and shoot to far distances, therefore, when you see a tank camp, it is very isolated. There was generally nothing around us in any direction, sometimes for hundreds of kilometres. There were other army camps, but we knew exactly where they were and they usually were behind a mountain range protected from the other camps.

Tanks camps are set in a U-shape with all the tanks facing outwards, ready to go. Each company would live right behind the tanks, so we could grab our stuff, jump on the tank and drive forward shooting. It is quite a powerful sight to see 30 odd tanks start their engines in the night, radio silence and go. It creates a huge dust storm as they disappear into the desert. The tanks grind the soil with their chains every day, so the ground around the tanks and outside was many times knee-deep fine dust. You don't want to drop anything there, as you would never find it again.

During that three-month intense course, you all rotate, all the time from driver to cannon, loader to commander. There is no one else to do it for you. You get to learn the team role very well and you develop an overall skill set that grooms you to become a commander. As much as I try and recall experiences from that period, it seems vague and lacks details.

Later on, in my army career, actually my last assignment in the army, I came back to the same camp as a captain in charge of training all future tank commanders in the north. I do remember my first encounter with a real desert. We were stationed somewhere deep in the desert, not far from the main mountain path that created a natural border with Egypt at the time. At that stage, Israel had already returned a portion of the Sinai Desert to Egypt. It allowed Egypt to regain control of the Suez Canal, which was the only shipping route between the Mediterranean Sea and Europe to Asia and India.

Oddly, the desert still reminds me of the ice. It's vastness, emptiness and raw beauty. It can be as deadly as the ice when temperatures can vary between -10°C at night to +50°. We used to train, sometimes, at over +50°C, exposed to the sun. It was a dry heat, so while we were losing fluids quickly, we didn't actually feel the sweat. We just had huge stains of dry salt under our armpits, tummy, groins and elsewhere. The dry sweat materialised as big white stains that looked like salt flakes on the surface. So, because of this, we had to hydrate non-stop. Many days were spent in a haze of dehydration, moving slowly, and looking for any possible shade. Unfortunately, the only shade we had was the shade of the tank, the briefing tent or inside the tank. Inside the tank, it felt like a dry sauna at around 60°C. We sucked water all the time, warm to hot water, we didn't care, but we needed to hydrate.

The trick to observing dehydration was pinching the skin on our arms. If it didn't go back quickly, it wasn't good. If the skin stayed erected and slowly, slowly settled back on the arm, we knew we were in trouble. Urinating was also a good test. As long as we needed to pass water, we knew we had some fluids in the system. When that dried out, we knew. It comes back to me as an almost surreal moment in my life, in comparison with the ice swimming, thinking about how we survived that. But then it was real and we were young. We simply adapted and carried on. Every now and then some lucky bugger managed to get an IV to revive him. But for that, you had to be seriously incapacitated.

Sunsets in the deserts were the most beautiful sight ever and they brought great relief from the scorching heat as they put the desert to bed in an amazing display of colours. The night was a completely different story. Temperatures dropped below zero sometimes and we weren't equipped for those radical conditions. If I had today's thermal gear, it would have been so different. But then we only had cotton socks. Nothing breathable. Our feet in the leather boots simply froze! Waking and running were fine as they kept the circulation going and kept us warm, but it was the stationery moments that almost killed us. It was one of the few times in my life that I looked forward to running. Generally, running was never my thing. Later on, I realised that my sports asthma played a big role in this, but back then, we knew nothing about it. I just knew that as we start running, my lungs shut down and I basically couldn't breathe. I would need to stop and just watch the others galloping around like antelopes.

Being in tanks, we spent many nights exercising with our beloved tank. The tanks, in fact, acted like a deep freeze. Massive layers of lead absorbed the icy cold air into its soul and dropped the temperature inside the tank even further. We would sit inside the tank, sometimes for hours, waiting for our time to exercise, while we felt like there was an icy wind blowing from inside the walls.

When in the tank commander's course, the focus was on each tank unit. We had very few exercises altogether and mostly, we split into two areas and practised one tank at a time. Tanks cover huge distances and spit multiple types of live ammunition at a 180 degrees angle from the right to left and the front. That forced all the rest to park far behind, safe and out of possible danger. The exercise part was active fun. We had to cover a tank obstacle course for several kilometres. Some obstacles were of landscape nature and we had to navigate through them and the others were of 'enemy' nature. Many times, they came together to make sure we are extremely busy.

It was an insane firepower machine; all live ammunition from our personal guns to large automatic machine guns mounted on the tank to small artillery, hand grenades and of course, the main guy, Mr 105 mm big cannon. This guy also spat various types of shells, sometimes 30m ahead, when being attacked by an enemy bazooka or RPG. In the night of the desert, with very limited eyesight, it was an orgy of firepower from a moving tank at high speed.

I just remember being so drained, covered with sweat yet on a massive high. It was a dangerous exercise, but we followed protocol and despite our severe lack of sleep, lack of eyesight and lack of experience, we were highly supervised by vast experience. And we followed protocol 100%! Not 99.99%. Anything below 100% was simply not acceptable.

A few years later, when I came back to the desert to commander position, there were a few hundred tanks moving through the dark spitting fire and spanning over 100 km. That was when things got a little more complicated. Mistakes were inevitable and people did get hurt, many from friendly fire. I was very lucky in avoiding getting hurt or hurting anyone in friendly fire. I do, however, remember, very clearly, one exercise, when we were deep into the night in the Sinai Desert. Targets were marked with small red lights linked to a battery. But in the middle of the night, identifying targets from 2 km to 4 km wasn't easy. Each tank had two red cat eyes on the back. Experience taught us to identify between various tanks' backs and fronts using the shape of the cat eyes, the distance between them and their distance from the ground among a few other tricks.

But that specific night, we were advancing, part of a massive formation spread across the desert. It was our time to advance and start covering the target in the distance. I saw a red light in the 'enemy' location that looked, to me, like a target in the distance. It wasn't straight ahead, but around 10 o'clock to the left. I could see it was stationary and looked ready for the picking. I got my cannon guy on the target, but for whatever reason, it just didn't look right. I couldn't get any verification with all the night vision and technology we had. And it just didn't feel right. No one was supposed to be ahead of us, but pitch-dark changes perspective. I decided to confirm on the radio if anyone was at that location. They confirmed there was no one. Finally, I asked the other unit that was supposed to be to the left of my unit to move a little. Finally, I saw the 'red light target' moving. We realised it was just another tank from another unit which advanced too quickly and wasn't supposed to be there. Phew! That had been a close one.

We weren't as lucky with the machine guns. Taking fire from another friendly tank happened occasionally. Usually, you saw the red trails rushing your way and it was a good sign to duck inside the tank and get everyone to cease fire on the radio. Later, a good officer friend ended up spending time in army jail for accidentally shooting down his officer friend at night. It was a mistake, middle of the night, dust, dark, dozens of tanks moving and spitting fire. I am not sure how he handled it, but I just know that he never spoke about it after he came out of jail. What a burden for a young 21-year-old man to carry with him for the rest of his life!

Friendly fire accidents in drills or action are common. It is not talked about a lot though. It was a taboo subject. I mean how do you tell the parents that his friend accidentally shot their child soldier? How sad.

Growing up in Israel and spending a few years in an active army hardens you a lot. It hardens the nation a lot. Everyone lost someone during the army or one of the wars. It was a reality. And not something everyone talks about all the time. You are not unique in your loss. You are lucky to grow old, have all your limbs intact, have good eyesight and are basically healthy. One of the hardest things ever was to tell the parents that their son, their young boy, was gone. We were so young, too young to understand any of this. It was simply the way things were and we adapted and dealt with it. But not everyone did.

Back to the desert at night, sitting in the tank with the air temperature dropping below zero and the tank acting as our freezer, we could be found covering our feet with newspapers and plastic bags. This was another hazy period for me.

When we got back to our camp, the work started. We had to service the tank, rinse the machine guns, collect all the empty shells and bring the tank back to ground zero, ready for action. This used to happen at around from 2 am to 4 am. We all moved like zombies between the tanks. We couldn't rush as we were just too tired. We had half-barrels filled with gun petrol and oil to wash the machine guns. Many times, it had a thin layer of ice on top. We used the machine gun to break the ice, then we would dip the machine gun in and out several times in this semi-frozen slush.

Following this, we would rush back to the tank, drop it on the back of the tank and rush to the showers to rinse our hands with warm water. It was my first encounter with frozen hands and the excruciating finger pain that follows. We had to grease the tanks chains and moving parts and while I can't remember how we managed, I just remember how dirty we were, stinking from a mixture of the day's dried sweat, petrol, oil, gunfire and grease. Yet, we mostly kept our sense of humour.

Besides that, we had a cabin with hot showers and as we finished, we all rushed to cleanse and warm up. The other guys in the camps, those working in the kitchen, laundry, and logistics, used to sneak into our showers when they ran out of hot water and used our hot water. Needless to say, we were furious. We would send a few warning messages, but one night, we came back at around 3 am frozen to the bones only to see steam pouring out of our shower windows. It was two guys from the laundry. So, we sneaked under the cabin and closed the hot water. Within a minute they rushed out butt naked, swearing and threatening to kill who was responsible for it. The next 30 minutes were not a pretty sight. The two guys ended up in the hospital. Suffice to say, they got hot showers but were immobile for a few weeks. But no one ever touched our hot water again. The story travelled a long distance in the desert, even to other camps. Needless to say, my company paid dearly for this action. We stood as a unit and paid for it as a unit. I can't say I am proud of our actions that night, but in the long run, no one got hurt and the lesson was loud and clear. Don't mess with another man's hot water in a frozen desert at 3 am in the morning.

Living in an environment like an active army pushes many to their limits. Suicide was also common news and very unwelcome. Since then, the army has changed a lot in terms of its understanding of the social and physical pressure it places on its soldiers, the Israeli army now is very different from what it was in my day. Nowadays, there are phones, email, mobile phones and social networks, all are useful as an outlet for depression and emotional issues, which normally arise. They can now identify these issues much earlier on and help the soldiers.

A couple of times as an officer on the border, I found myself at the end of another desperate soldier's machine gun, screaming and on the verge of losing it. I managed to calm him down. I was lucky once again, it seemed. In the Golan Heights on the border, in my tank unit, the regiment commander was even luckier. The tank camp was set in a U-shape, where each leg of the U-shape was a line of tanks facing outwards, with around ten tanks on each leg. Behind each leg of ten tanks were our barracks. The barracks were literally a few meters away, so when needed, we simply picked our stuff up and ran outside, climbed on the tank and moved forward. It required firing forward in three directions. It was quite a sight to see 30 tanks moving outwards quietly at night and firing their canons. You certainly don't want to be caught on the outside of that.

The regiment headquarter was stationed in the middle of the U, protected. It had the headquarters room, office and two tanks. This was where the regiment commander and his second in command stayed.

I want to take a step back to explain how the tank starts. Usually, it is the easiest to climb up from the front, where it is the lowest part of the tank and is accessible. The driver cabin is open and the first one jumping on the tank sticks his hand inside the driver cabin, searching for the 24V switch. We all knew how to find it with our eyes closed. It was a second habit and it happened automatically. Once the switch was on, everything worked in the tank. The driver slots in and starts the tank and everyone follows radio orders. Mr 105 mm cannon was always lowered down, resting on the left side of the tank pointing down. The driver's cabin was on the right, so the cannon must leave the cabin door uncovered. The cannon was also lowered down, resting, to avoid unnecessary pressure on the mechanism operating the cannon. This could have led to erosion of the moving parts and could lead to reduced accuracy.

Now, one evening, an electrician climbed up the regiment commander's tank to run some tests. It was pitch dark and he climbed up from the front, sticking his hand inside the driver's cabin, searching for the 24V switch. As he was about to click it up, he noticed that the cannon was not resting on the left side. It was actually closer to the centre, parallel to the ground, pointing somewhere. It was not common and it does happen that the crew forgets to place the cannon in its resting place and position. The cannon was also making it slightly difficult to reach the 24V switch.

The technician decided to climb up and check the cannon. As he climbed into the tank, reaching for the manual handle to lower down the cannon, he noticed that the cannon trigger, which is situated on the handle, was clicked in with tape. That raised his suspicion. He decided to check the cannon and as he looked through the periscope, he saw the target cross dead straight on the regiment commander's office. He checked to find if there was a live shell in the canon. Had he followed the automatic procedure and clicked up the 24V switch, the cannon would have fired a live shell into the regiment commander's office. It was only around 20 m away, but it would have demolished the entire building and whoever habituated it. We never found out who did this. But clearly, someone was seriously unhappy with our colonel.

The course continued in a sleepless haze of icy cold, extreme heat and lots of greases. Needless to say, that food was not a product of a master chef or to be more accurate, any chef. It was basic, mostly tasteless and cold. We didn't have much time to down the food and nothing to snack with. We did get parcels from home though. The parcels and letters came once a week. Post dispensing was a humiliating process. We all had to line up, with the corporal reading the names on each letter including the name of the senders. Any envelope of colour, scent or even worse, with a few hearts and kisses on it cost us push-ups. The more pink and hearts were on the envelopes the more push-ups.

But besides that, the parcels were sent from heaven or to be precise, our mothers. Generally, they contained cigarettes, cake and some food that was considered a delicacy at the time. The correct process was to open your parcel, take out the personal stuff and place it in the middle of the tent for all to feast on. But every team had their biscuit mouse. The ones that left a near-empty parcel in public only to eat their biscuits inside the safety of their sleeping bag late at night. None of them escaped our hungry ears and when found, the food was confiscated and placed somewhere for everyone. My elder brother, Hemi, was also in tanks and used to spend his camps in reserves, not far from me. Thankfully, he used to pop in sometimes and bring me some burgers and chocolates.

The army continued and I finished my tank commander's course with flying colours and by some miracle managed to avoid any trouble with our officers. That hasn't lasted for long though in my everyday life. We were sent home for 48 hours of leave, the only time I was allowed to wear my tank commander, the three stripes on the side of my shoulder, a corporal ('samal' in Hebrew). After a year in the army, I finally had some rank and 'respect', well, for 48 hours at least, before heading straight for nine months of officer's course. Again, no rank, no privileges, kak food and just do!

As mentioned, in the Israeli army, unlike most armies, conscription is compulsory, minimum of three years for men and two years for women. Everyone starts at the bottom. Everyone starts at the same place, regardless of their education, capabilities and any relationships with anyone in power. These things help to get one into certain units, such as the air force, navy or other elite units. But when you walk in, you start at the bottom. You learn to be a proper soldier before you can command anyone and get handed over huge responsibilities. The army invests hugely in officers and it takes around two years, sometimes more, to graduate as a junior officer. This way, officers are made to sign for extra time in the army as the army wants to ensure a return on its investment.

I was sent to another desert this time, placed in the Negev, south of Jerusalem. It is a different desert to Sinai, smaller, rich with history yet still a desert. The first three months of the officer's course were a multi-army course in a place called in Hebrew Bahad 1. No tanks, just an officer's basic course. For the first time in the army, we actually had rooms, proper rooms with beds and showers. We felt like royalty. We had lectures in large rooms and we were in a very interesting company. I shared a room with navy seals, commando fighters and a helicopter pilot. What a melting pot. We worked very well together and learnt a lot. It was the first time that things actually started to make sense to me. Not war and politics, I was too young for that, but the actual structure of the army, strategy, tactics and how it actually worked. We all had books to read, compulsory books about Napoleon, Alexander the great, the Battle of Stalingrad and other army leaders many years ago. The theoretical stuff came easy to me. Strategy, tactics, planning, and execution were quite straightforward to me.

But the running with 20 kg to 30 kg of various stuff on top of me never became easier. I had no problem marching with any amount of weight on me, but the minute we started running, I was left behind. I recall an obstacle course in the Wingate sports academy near Tel Aviv on the beach, a place where many army units trains. We had to do what was called "the death obstacle course", as it was called. It was a very long obstacle course, in the sand, by the beach, in the sea. It included a long run in the sand and many fascinating obstacles like walking in the sea waves, chest high with your gun and 20kg-30kg all up above your head. It wasn't the usual course we always did at camp as it was around five times longer and took fewer hours.

During the process, you wished you were dead, many times. We had all our gear on and we started with a run in the sand. We were sent in heats of ten and within a minute I was left way behind the group. For me the run was all about survival, slowly but surely, I had to do it. Once it was over, the obstacles started. That was the easy part as I was light, had strong arms and could climb like a monkey. I started passing my teammates. I remember one huge and strong guy was stuck by the rope. All you had to do was climb up five metres, touch the top and slide down with all your gear. The poor guy just stood there in near tears, trying again and again. Gravity was simply not going to let him up that rope. Later on, I passed another fast runner who couldn't drag himself above a small swamp hanging on a rope. He kept on falling and starting again. It was all about strategy.

Young officer

I knew my strengths and many limits. I knew I would have to dig really deep to survive the run, but I also knew that the rest was within my reach. It was not the first time in my life I had seen big men built like Greek gods but crying like kids. I focused on my mental strength, I knew I was no Greek god, but more like a snooker cue, I knew I had to recruit all I had to survive there. The army never broke me nor humiliated me. I learnt that your mind is the strongest muscle in your body and it can grow, learn and get stronger.

The officer's course wasn't as hard as the previous courses, maybe because it was starting to get mentally stimulating and challenging and finally, I was using some brain, not just brawn. But that made me drop my guards down and allowed that little red guy with the two horns and mischievous personality sitting on my left shoulder to wake up. The officers running the course were all well-known army generals and later on, some of them commanded the north or south of the army and some even ended up as chief of the army and in politics.

Although we were treated with much more respect than in previous courses, we were cadets and discipline was extremely strict, in fact, many were expelled regularly. Once a week, the generals had an expulsion meeting. If your name was put forward for expulsion by one of the generals, they would discuss your case and 95% of the time, you were out. My name was discussed twice! I was never great with authority. Today, I am not sure how I made it through the other side. But that's in many ways the story of my life.

The first time, I was on guard duty somewhere in the desert. We were all staying in small tents, two cadets per tent, and I was extremely tired and extremely cold. My tent mate was to replace me and the rules were that you had to wake him up and continue patrolling until he replaced you. Many times, they would fall asleep again and you had to keep on going back to try and kick them out of bed. When you have had four to six hours of sleep a night with two hours of guard duty, every minute is as dear as gold. So, I woke up my tent mate and decided to sit down in the tent and make sure he got up. While he was dressing up, I was dressing down, planning to tuck into my sleeping bed exactly on the hour, leaving no room for wastage, every second of sleep counted.

As I started taking off my shoes, the chief general opened my tent. He was looking for the guard and saw a light in one of the tents. He literally caught me with my pants down. As I saw his face, I knew this was the end. Getting caught breaching guard duty was an automatic jail sentence in the army and not just expulsion. Now I had, and still do, the ability to switch my fear off when fate is staring me in the eyes. There was nothing to do, no lies or stories could cover this one up and so, I got out, told him the truth and he walked away. I spent the week knowing that that was it. I was out. I know my name was discussed, but I also know I hadn't been expelled yet and I had no idea why. The gods must have favoured me or maybe I got points in strategic thinking.

The second time was not as serious as an army no-no, but I was very naughty. We were part of a huge drill in the desert. In the officer's course, we had no soldiers as we played every role, so sometimes you had to act as an officer and sometimes you had to be a foot soldier, which was clearly the boring part. My team was stationed on top of a cliff surrounding a dry river path low below us. It was an ambush and I had a small role to play but only at some stage later on in the afternoon. I was the unlucky one, facing the other direction for potential risks with no real role at all. My best mate at the time, who was a special forces unit fighter, was also quite mischievous and once the shooting started, he called me over to where the action was just before I fell asleep.

Everyone was shooting from all over the place, in all directions, at the 'kill zone', which was down below us. The right way is to shoot two rounds at a time unlike in the movies, where they shoot as if ammunition is never an issue. My gun had 35 live rounds, so Oded, my mate, challenged me to empty the 35 rounds with one finger squeeze. If you have never used a gun before (and good for you), it takes a while to squeeze the finger for 35 rounds non-stop. I was always game for an interesting challenge, so I aimed and squeezed. Suddenly, in this concert of single bang-bang, you heard this never-ending stream of bangs 35 times.

As I emptied my magazine, everyone stopped, looking in my direction. There was this eerie silence and no one knew what had happened. My officer ran towards me, as red as a cooked lobster, and ordered me to wait by the truck in the back. Later on, he came and screamed his heart out at me. Again, I knew I was dead and that expulsion was imminent. However, interestingly enough, the officer felt much better after bursting out at me. He asked me what on earth came on me and I answered the truth. I just had to try it and see what it was like. Again, no idea how, but I survived that one as well.

Later on, when I went to the senior officer's course, I was told at the awards ceremony by the general heading the course, "Barkai, you were considered for an A. You were also considered for the top award in the course for your performance, however, one of the generals brought up an incident, where you told him exactly what you thought of him. Therefore, you get D in the discipline, which takes your overall mark to AB or A-." And that is the price of telling people what you think of them. I was 100% fine with that. I did what I did, rightfully so, and paid the price with my head up. The story of my life. That story is coming later.

After the first part of the multinational officer's course, we were all sent back to our respective units to continue specialising as officers in tanks, air force, navy and so on. I went straight back to the Sinai Desert for another six months. Back to the dust, grease, heat and freezing cold. Again, although we were soon to become officers, we had no soldiers but us. We spent our training alternating between driving tanks, loading canons and training as officers. It was at that time that I realised that I suffered from partial dyslexia. I also found out that most people hide it and are embarrassed about it. Later on, I also found out that I 'have' various other mild issues and most people in the world have several mild disorders. Actually, I learnt not to trust perfect people because I never knew what kind of issues they could be hiding and when they would materialise. I learnt to respect people who wore their issues like they wear socks and shoes and got on with life with the dice rolled for them. Maybe one scary day, we will be able to pick the gene cocktail that makes us. Then we will all be 100% perfect and 200% boring.

Back to dyslexia. As an officer, you start giving commands on the external radio frequency, guiding other tanks. There are a clear set of rules and vocabulary to execute such communication. I started to realise that I was confusing left and right quite comfortably. Looking right, aiming right and commanding left. I still do it in my car sometimes but thank God for Google maps and GPS. I learnt very quickly that the best way to deal with such a thing was to acknowledge it, not deny the issue and learn to correct my actions accordingly. It is not easy. People, yes, even grown-ups, can mock and bully other grown-ups for their mild disorders, unaware of what is actually going on inside that person's brain and how they are dealing with such a handicap. And even though it was mild, it was still a daily nuisance. Regardless of that, from the adversary comes strength. In my mind, every disadvantage opens a door to new opportunities that were not there for you before. My mind worked fast, corrected and reacted very quickly and I didn't panic!

Much later on in life, I visited the University of Bloemfontein in South Africa. I was then the CEO of the very successful Cadiz Holdings, a listed financial services company. They took us to a faculty for students with various impairments. There was one guy that attracted my attention. He was blind and was working on his computer, using special software and a keyboard. He had headphones on and every mouse click and movement translated into sounds of words in his ears. The software and the technology were new to me, but what blew my mind most was the fact that that student was listening to everything at three times the normal speed, which made his operation of the computer seem normal.

I remember asking him if I could listen only to discover that all I could hear was 'speedy Gonzales talking' (Google it). It was a fast-squeaky voice at such a speed that I couldn't make sense of anything. When I asked him about it, he chuckled. His blindness had reduced a lot of sensory noise and allowed him to develop a fantastic hearing ability. I am sure he would have given it all back to get his sight back, but it was just an example of how disadvantages can create some new opportunities.

Another area where I exploited a disadvantage into an advantage was when I realised I could focus, really focus, if I applied my mind to it. When I needed to focus, I simply shut down most noise around me and created a quiet shield around me. I still do this to date and my kids know when I am busy and focused, I am in another space regardless of all the noise around me.

So, back to the army. I started to listen to several radio frequencies all at one time. The main frequency was the internal radio where we communicated inside the tank. Then there was the company frequency, the one we used to command the tanks around us and finally there was the regiment frequency where orders were issued to the captains. I learnt to distinguish between the frequencies even though sometimes, it all came as mangled spaghetti into my ears. I actually enjoyed it.

A quick rest on the back of my tank in Sinai desert, me in the middle

Aside from the hectic training and many memories, or shades of memories, I had specific memories, usually naughty ones. One such memory was when our greasing machine broke down at 3 am. We were tired, cold and extremely low on a sense of humour. I went round to wake up someone in the logistics area to give us another machine. It was very dark at the gate and I stood there shouting my lungs out trying to wake up the man in charge. We weren't liked much at that stage. We were cadets and that was the time the private could still exercise their power when they had the opportunity. Later on, when we became officers, things changed.

So, at the gate, the grease machine guy told me to take a walk using some flowery vocabulary. His excuse was that his officer didn't allow the use of those spare machines and he couldn't give us one. I told him to tell his officer to shove his greasing machine up his wide backside. Needless to say, I was court marshalled the next day for my wrong use of words and lost a long-anticipated leave for another six weeks.

The top two cadets are required to stay behind for nine months and continue as officers training new cadets. It was a great honour and I got to wear a special black stripe with rank. I also got a lot of respectful glares when I travelled home.

A few months after the course finished, I ended up at one first officer's dinner, sitting next to a senior officer, who was telling everyone about a cheeky cadet who had told him to shove his greasing machine where the sun didn't shine. I turned to my left and told him it was me. We had a drink, and a laugh and became great friends after that. I did, however, apologise and told him it was just an expression of anger and that I never really expected him to follow my demand.

I finished my officer's course and was extremely proud. Most people in the kibbutz thought I would spend my life in an army jail remembering my naughty youth. Instead, I finished top of my course. My dad's health was getting very frail by that stage and he lost all his hardness just as I was starting to get close to him as an adult. As a child, I didn't get to know him very well. He was a difficult person, but I always knew he loved us.

We were allowed to invite two family members to the graduation ceremony. The army flew them from Tel Aviv to the Sinai Desert as it was not a place you could get to on your own. I flew with my dad and my girlfriend at the time and I had never seen my dad so proud in all my life. I think he probably had rescaled his expectations of me after my turbulent teenage days and being expelled from high school. Sadly, he died a couple of months after that and I will always remember him in the desert, in the heat and the dust with all the tanks around him. And his son, as an officer, was so proud and so happy.

A few months later, I left home again, back to the desert as an officer in the same course. My father had just had another heart attack and it was Saturday, just before I had to go back to the army. I visited him in the hospital and he looked fine. I had gotten used to seeing him in ICU with all the machines and pipes and we would crack a joke, following which I would say goodbye and that I would see him in two weeks.

As an officer, we were allowed to fly to Sinai and back, a huge luxury that saved us a 12-hour bus trip. I would arrive at the camp late at night and we would then have to prepare everything for the next morning, an early start.

Around midday, during a live exercise, we received a call from the general. It was on the radio like any other communication as there were no cell phones or any personal devices back then. Everyone could hear everything. I was asked to come back immediately to the camp and it was a very unusual request. We were not on border duty, so nothing usually requires such urgency. But as I put the radio down, I knew. I left the camp immediately. After an hour of dusty driving at 50°C and I didn't dare to ask anything on the radio, but I knew. When I arrived, I went straight to his office and he broke the news to me, "Your father has passed away." After I had left home, he had deteriorated during the night. My brother, Amos, had been with him all night, but he knew what was coming. My mother was in Tel Aviv for work and at some stage, a decision he made was to call her as my father kept on asking for her and my brothers realised that the end was near. My father hung in there on a thin thread until my mother arrived to pass away only a few minutes after her arrival. I was 21 years old at the time and my younger brother, Yair, was just 11 years old.

The army continued, and after nine months as an officer in officer's course, I was finally sent back to the Golan Heights. Home! I was a senior officer already, had my own Jeep and an office and of course my tank. I was the regiment operations officer, working closely with the colonel, so close that his secretary became my girlfriend, well, for a wee while.

We were by the Syrian border, and we had a lot of work, but it was a 30-minute drive from home. I could pop in, sometimes late at night, to visit my mother and reload on some food. My friends were all in the army. Life was very different. The Golan Heights was a busy place, but we could go out some evenings to restaurants. Alcohol was a strict no-no but also not desired. It was only later on in my life that I realised that I really caught up on life because I never touched alcohol.

Within a few months, I attained my first company. A company is the first autonomous unit in the army. As a company commander, you get your own camps, kitchen, drivers, medics, technical stuff and Personal Assistance. There I was, 22 years old with around 12 tanks, 50 soldiers, a few other vehicles and my own camp. So much power, so young and with so much responsibility.

Life on the Syrian border was never boring. It was a very jittery life on the border, especially being so close to home. I was a hard captain and I always took the responsibility very seriously, at times too seriously, but it was also the norm. We were young and very proud of ourselves. We were too young to understand politics and have the perspective we developed later, yet I still remember one night, after spending 24 hours in our tanks on the border, ready to go. The radio was silent, we were in position with hundreds of tanks. There was such firepower ready to ignite with just one word from the radio. However, around 3 am, the order came to go back to camp. It was slightly disappointing and we didn't sleep for a few nights after that, being kept up on the adrenaline, cigarettes and coffee we had consumed prior to the raid. This was our staple diet.

I recall my young soldiers, all-around 19 years of age, so disappointed as if someone had pulled the plug on an exciting race at the start line. So, I assembled everyone at 4 am to give them a lecture about life, as I am known to do sometimes. I told them about the paradox of being trained to do our job yet being denied from doing it. I told them how lucky we were, in fact, not to have to go through that night. There is nothing pretty about war. It is a horrible experience that needs to be avoided at all costs. And if you have no choice, never indulge in a war of any kind. In fact, try to do away with it as soon as possible. I hope that a politician reads this.

I was sent to a senior officer's course in the centre and it was a great course. We had officers from various other armies around the world and we even had a few South African captains, who used to iron their uniforms every day. I found that hilarious. In the Israeli army, if you had done that, you would not have been considered a real soldier. Neat was not the look we were after. You could identify commando fighters from a distance as they used to be able to get away with any look; unshaven, rough shorts with a shirt hanging out and generally a mess. The Israeli army was significantly less formal than any other army I saw. However, there was respect, always respect and communications were very open and based on respect rather than authority. It created excellent teamwork in times of need. There were very little luxuries in the army or at least in the army I had experienced. No officers party or gala dinner, no clubs, bars or many privileges, just lots and lots of responsibility and at a very young age. It is the way I have been brought up, but it certainly has its price.

The course was very interesting. This time, we had soldiers operating the tanks. We actually had plenty of time to study and practice, but it was a high level of exercise. We had officers from all over the army and it was, in fact, great fun. Every drill had an air force or a navy. We had the crème de la crème training us. Needless to say, I did very well and got into serious trouble as well. There were long hot days of multi-army exercises and sometimes, we were assigned a colonel role and sometimes a sergeant role as someone had to do it. I was assigned a jeep and a flag at the back, driving in a convoy for hours in the heat.

Later on, I was called to go back to the desert for six months to head the tank commander's courses as I was a seasoned officer by then. When orders are given on the radio, a tank commander confirms this by raising a flag. One only confirms on the radio when asked to do so. When an order was given, I would raise my right hand to signal – confirmed. I remember one incident when, from nowhere, one of the generals, a very famous general from the 1973 war, barked at me personally on the regiment radio. My code was A1 and he said, "A1 when the general gives an order, you confirm with a flag!" I looked around, I couldn't find my flag and raised my hand again.

What I didn't realise, was that that general was right next to me. He stopped my jeep and started screaming at me. I had never exchanged words with him before till then. He was called tiger, which was his code name in the 1973 war, and he was very famous for his boldness and the textbook ambush that he executed on a Syrian division with only a few tanks. But I had not known that he was arrogant and rude. So, I did exactly what he would have done. I didn't lower my eyes and apologise. Instead, I told him that whoever used the jeep before me took the flags and anyways, I was way behind, invisible, so I used my hand. I also saw it imperative to tell him that that doesn't require him to be so rude. Needless to say, I was simply pouring oil onto the fire. He summarily decided to expel me but luckily, he found out later that I did extremely well on the course and my general managed to calm him down. It was such a Deja vu… which continued in my entire life. I simply can't tolerate bullying or brazen arrogance.

It was not the first time I had met huge egos in the army. I also met strong and forceful commanders, but I had no respect for arrogance. Yes, I also used my power in the army, but I was always very careful to be fair and never arrogant. I saw famous generals stripping soldiers of their rank because they dared not to listen while they were talking about their greatness. I sent people to jail several times and punished my soldiers many times, but I had a strict rule – 'every punishment had to be strictly linked to the reason and had to have an intelligent lesson and fairness attached to it.'

My last stint in the army was back in the desert for six months. It was strange going back to a place you remembered from your basic tank training but as a senior commanding officer. I knew then that I had to get out of the army. I was 23 years old and I felt like a 50-year-old. The responsibility was way too much and I needed to get back to real life, have fun, and get back to my water. I was very flattered by the effort they made to try and convince me to stay, but my mind was made up. For whatever reason, I was very good at it. I got promoted very quickly all the time. I found the army easy, simple and uncomplicated. But I knew I couldn't keep on going on two packets of cigarettes a day, a few jars of coffee and adrenaline. Later on, I stopped smoking, cut down on coffee and replaced those vices with whiskey and ice.

After a few weeks, I was suddenly, again, a young kid, a high school dropout, but with a major rank in tanks. Not much experience in anything else, but I was free again.

Chapter 4
The Fire

Suddenly, seemingly out of nowhere, a breeze tickled the back of my neck and for a second, I received it with great relief as it was so hot out. I relished in it again as I realised that hell had just opened its gates.

It was a 'normal' boiling day in the Jordan Valley, around 40°C, with not a breath of wind and clear skies. Mid-May 1980, saw me finishing my five years of service in the Israeli army. I had started to grow my hair again, was working in the fields and had got back to a normal and simple life; a life filled with no real responsibilities. I was healthy, had four limbs, two eyes, no significant scars to boast about and was raring to restart my life. In Israel, after five years of mostly border service in the Golan Heights or the Sinai Desert, being healthy and intact was considered lucky.

So, there I was, sitting in my tractor, driving in first gear in the middle of a harvested wheat field, dragging behind me a tank of water with a long metal wire attached to it. The wire was linked to a burning tyre. They were low flames as tyres are very flammable and burn for a long time.

The reason for the burning tyre was as follows. After the harvest, the field is left with short stubble about five inches long and the stubble that the combine harvester doesn't catch because it can't cut too close to the ground is finished off by the burning tyre. This stubble blunts the discos when you turn the soil around for the next season and the best way to get rid of it was to burn it with fire. As mentioned, it was a super-hot day and May can be one of the hottest months in the Jordan Valley. It was the *Hamssin* (an Arabic word for extreme heat with no wind) season with a scorching sun and not a breath of wind for days. We usually got the blessed west thermal wind in the afternoon, which blew the heat away and brought the desired wind that we, as avid windsurfers, grew to love. But in May, the heat could go on for days.

Regardless, I had to drive very slowly. One, to make sure that the tyre burned the hay stubble properly and two, to avoid flying sparks. The field was cornered between the main road on one side and fields on the other three sides. The field to the west was ready to be harvested hayfield, high yellow dry stems, top-heavy with grains and erecting around one and a half meters. One spark and that field would erupt like an oil field in this heat. I had a young kid working with me and he was running around as my gopher gathering new tyres to burn, fetching water and generally being on fire alert.

I was driving east on the field about 20 m from the next wheat field and a narrow gravel road separated the harvested field and the need to be harvested field. The wind was channelling from the west, behind me, and it picked up rapidly. At one point, I looked back and realised I would have to pack up very quickly or the fire would carry over with the wind to the neighbouring fields. I knew the westerly wind very well and it would come from nowhere, picking up to 30 knots within minutes. I was looking around, shouting for the youngster working with me, but I couldn't see him. Looking forward, my worst nightmare started unfolding before my very eyes. The wind carried some sparks across the field and the edge of the other wheat field was catching fire.

I didn't think. I put off the fire on the burning tyre and drove straight into the wheat field, positioning myself ahead of the flames around 20 m. I left the engine on and jumped off the tractor, running to the water tanker I was towing behind me. As I was about to pick up the hosepipe and open the water, I saw this tsunami of fire rushing towards me. The field was on fire and with the wind picking up, it carried the fire like an avalanche, increasing in size every metre.

The next few events happened very quickly. I have tried many times since then, to replay it in my memory. Could or should I have done something differently? Did I panic? How big was the fire? I have a vague memory of how things happened and I realised then that I had to run for my life or I would be roasted alive.

The firewall that rushed towards me was much taller than I and it was close, very close. I had to run. But I couldn't leave the tractor to burn there or I would never have been able to show my face again in my kibbutz. It was a big blue Ford, relatively new, so the choice was easy. I ran to the tractor and tried to push it into gear knowing that if I panicked, it will stall. I could feel the heat on my body to the point that it was unbearable. I tried to shift the gear into first, but all I was met with was a horrible grinding noise of metal teeth refusing the engage. Before I knew it, the fire was upon me and I could feel it burning my right side. I could smell the back of my hair catching fire and I smacked it with my right hand to put it out.

The gear finally engaged and the tractor moved forward. I drove off away from the fire as there was nothing I could do to stop it. I clearly needed to get help. As I drove towards the main road, I could smell the distinguished scent of burning flesh, my flesh. I was wearing a sleeveless vest and I looked down at my right arm finding that I had no skin on my upper limb. There was just a red exposed gash. Luckily, I was in some kind of shock or focused otherwise as I'm sure I would have fainted. My skin was burnt terribly and folded down like a plastic sheet in a pile by my elbow. The exposed scar, when touched, still feels like I am in the middle of that fire.

I bashed the back of my head and my clothes with my hands, just in case something was still on fire but could feel that my face was burnt, my back and some part of my leg. My saving grace, for the rest of my body, was that I was wearing heavy field shoes and long trousers.

I eventually made it to the main road where cars were speeding by as if nothing wrong was happening. The fire was a few hundred meters away from the road and no one seemed to notice or have an inclination to act on it. Stopping the tractor on the side of the road, I started to panic about the youngster that was working with me and I shouted his name out. I couldn't see him anywhere. The one thing I did know was that I had to get to a hospital as soon as I could. I have had plenty of injuries in my life but nothing as bad as that. I couldn't move properly but attempted to lift my arm and flag down a car. The cars just ignored me, but I must admit, I wasn't a pretty sight. So, I walked straight into the middle of the road, facing the traffic and lifted my arms to my side just standing there. Soon someone had to stop. To my amazement, some cars just drove around me, probably not aware of my condition. But finally, a white car stopped and I opened the back door climbing in, shouting at them, "Take me to the hospital!"

The driver and passenger were both from one of the neighbouring farms, which were on the way to the co-op. My army training came in handy at that moment and I just started to give them orders. "Flash your lights!" and "Open the windows!" I felt like I was inside a boiling pot of fire. I then shouted, "Close the windows!" as the wind on my exposed flesh was unbearable. I explained to them that I had caught fire, but that I couldn't find the young boy who had been working with me.

I 'ordered' them to stop at the co-op so I could call my kibbutz and tell them that the field had caught fire. It was 1980 and of course, there were no mobile phones available. So, I repeated my story over the phone and further told them the tractor was on the side of the road.

I was practically jumping up and down trying to control my reaction to the unbearable pain. I needed something to alleviate the sting and I needed it very soon or I was going to go mad. If you didn't know, when you catch fire, your skin continues to burn even after it is out of the fire. It turned out that 20% of my body was burnt to various degrees. I was literally on fire and I could feel it. Twenty minutes later, after a simulated action movie car chase with me as the back-seat driver, we arrived at the hospital.

The following few days, weeks and months were another journey for me, a journey of pain and recovery. But I would get back again soon. That journey taught me much about life, pain and how to deal with it. This was my first encounter with fire and to this day I don't talk about it much and in fact, most of my friends have no idea or don't realise what actually happened to me back then. I don't like to dwell in my misery or the past unless it was good fun. That certainly was not!

Later on, the guys in the kibbutz decided to name that field, that caught fire, "Field Ram". Every field in the kibbutz has a name and it is usually called A1, B23 and so on. The field, some years later, became a mango plantation and as far as I am aware, it is still referred to as Ram. That was the first time a piece of the earth had been named after me. The second time it happened was in Antarctica and it was linked to ice.

I was rushed into the emergency room, stripped of my burnt clothes and covered with a clean white sheet. They lathered my burnt body surface with some white cream and left me in a quiet room. As I lay there, the reality of the recent events started to sink in. I had a moment to recap, rewind and watch that surreal movie of fire and how it had engulfed me. That didn't last for long though. The pain started to dominate every thought I tried to venture into. If you have ever experienced a tiny little skin burn on your finger, hands or elsewhere, they are usually first or second-degree burns. And you will know that they hurt like hell. My body, with its varying degrees of burns, from first to third, was pretty much unbearable. The pain enveloped me in its thick dark blanket and I couldn't take it anymore. I burst out of the room and demanded to be given some kind of painkillers or injection at the least.

I had been in the army for five years and I knew a little bit about pain treatment drugs. Finally, some doctor pulled out the magic needle and introduced me to what was to become my new best friend for the following two weeks – Pethidine, a close relative of morphine but much nicer and stronger. I was wheeled into a separate room, just for me. My last thought before succumbing to blissful sleep was that at least I was in business class and not the economy.

I found out later that fresh burns pose a huge risk of infection. When one has a huge body surface with no skin to protect you, a little infection can turn a surface burn into a deep crater and a whole different set of risks. The first 48 hours were a haze of drug-induced sleep and I would wake up every three hours as the drug effect faded, reeling in pain again. I couldn't move much and had to lay on my back covered with plenty of creams and bandages.

I recall my mom popping in, but she was always so worried and stressed, like a typical Jewish mom, that she was more of a liability to me and didn't help me relax at all. I ended up having to calm her down through my drug haze and told my brother later, "Mom is not allowed here until I feel better to handle her please." Only a few days later when I had accumulated enough courage to look in the mirror, did I realise why everyone looked so shocked when they visited me. The entire right side of my face was ashen black with skin missing in many areas. The fire had predominantly hit me on my right side, so I looked a lot like Two-Face from the *Batman* series, it was such a clear divide. My right ear was hanging like melted plastic, almost shapeless. My face was so swollen that I could hardly open my eyes to see. My nose and lips, especially on the right side of my face, were not attractive at all, to put it mildly.

After two days, we moved from injections to pills. Pethidine, like all severe pain drugs, is highly addictive and shouldn't be used for prolonged periods. Within two days, I knew each pill, dosage and its look and feel. I am an explorer, so I tested everything until I found something that worked well and that they would let me take.

For the following week, I was still encased in drugged heaven. I remember friends coming to visit and would be chilled and 'pain-free' for a few hours, but I would start to sense when the painkillers were starting to wear off. I knew exactly how long I would have before my sense of humour failed and would tell my friends, "Time to go." I would be already twitching in pain and looking at the clock counting the minutes for my next dose.

After a week, the nerves on my right arm, where I had the third-degree burns, started to wake up. Basically, the fire burnt all the surface nerves away and they took a while to grow back. No one had warned me about this, so I didn't see it coming. My brother, Amos, and his wife, Revi, were sitting quietly in my room studying for university, just to keep me company. I started to complain about the increased pain, which eventually became unbearable. The sensation was as if someone had thrown me into the fire again. The painkillers, that for the past few days had taken me into a wonderful chilled place, were rendered useless. I had no idea what was going on. I just knew I needed to see my old friend, Pethidine, as soon as possible. My poor brother and his wife had no idea what was going on either. They just knew I couldn't handle the pain anymore. I was sobbing like a child as they took me for a walk that evening. I simply lost control and any dignity or pride I may have been harbouring. I felt as if I was in the middle of the fire again and there was no one to help me out.

When I reflect on those painful hours, I wonder how would I deal with it now? Has the ice and my crazy adventure swims hardened me enough to handle such pain better? I have no idea. It was such a long time ago and I was much younger. For a long time, I felt ashamed of my behaviour, and my complete loss of control and I am certain that that specific evening had a huge impact on me, somewhere deep in my mental being.

Amos eventually gave up as he couldn't bear to see me like that. He left and somehow managed to convince them to put me back on the Pethidine. I don't remember much about the two days following. I was mostly floating somewhere between the injections on a cloud of oblivion.

After around ten days, the treatment started to settle down and I was getting into a routine. I still took painkillers for many months to follow, but it was more under control since I was scared of developing any addiction or dependency upon them. The hospital is not a great place to spend a long time. Everyone there is suffering from something and where I was, it was mostly serious. Some people just disappeared after a time but most got better. I made a mission to meet people and listen to their stories as it really helped to put my self-pity into perspective. It played a huge role in my recovery, mentally and physically. I was in the 'steak-ward', as I used to call it because everyone there had come there from a fire in some form or another.

Fire burns are huge surface injuries and when they start to recover, your skin literally comes back to life. So, if you have ever had a skin wound that forms a scab and starts to itch, you will have a small idea of what we fire survivors were going through. Think about 20% or more of your entire body being ravished by a tingling urge to scratch. The side effect was no sleep and even though we were all on some form of sleeping pills, you would find us wandering up and down the empty corridors of the steak-ward, restless and sleepless.

A room down the corridor had two young kids around seven or eight years old, who had been caught in a gas bottle explosion on their holiday. Their little faces were something from a horror show, but their spirits were high. I have no idea how or where they got that positive attitude, but it smacked me back into reality and I drew a lot of encouragement from them.

The healing process was long and unpleasant and I had to stay away from the sun for more than six months. I had to practically adopt a vampire lifestyle, sleeping during the day and walking around or keeping myself busy during the nights. It was the middle of summer, near the Sea of Galilee and temperatures were usually above 30°C, so the night became my friend.

I was very lucky and my skin healed extremely well. The doctors considered all types of skin grafts and I clearly remember a meeting when the doctors were talking about grafting skin off my arse to fix my right arm. Needless to say, I wasn't going to let anyone near my arse with a sharp object! Whether it was due to my darker skin tone, my luck or my destiny, I recovered really well without it. The doctors couldn't believe it and before I knew it, I was back to normal life after six months.

It did take a while for me to be able to spend time in the sun again though. I had to have a lot of physiotherapies to stretch the new skin and get my arm back to full span for movement. It is hardly noticeable anymore and doesn't place any limitations on my life. Fire is not my best friend, but I learnt to manage it and it doesn't bother me that much. The shrinks kept on asking me about nightmares and other psychological impacts, but I was 100% fine and still am.

Once I was healthy again and had my freedom back, I just moved on. I knew I had a very strong mind already, but the unplanned adventure in the fire taught me a lot and still comes back to teach me how to deal with pain mentally.

Many people have asked me, "How did you get into ice swimming?" I must admit, I have always looked at my life as a sequence of random events and I let life take me where it wants. I am not saying I am a passenger, not at all. I am most definitely the driver, well, most of the time, but I do like new adventures. Yes, admittedly the fire had something to do with it as well. I certainly don't like heat and only in recent years, have I managed to get my body into a sauna but only for short periods. I struggle with a hot environment and non-moving air. I feel claustrophobic in the heat, which is quite ironic too, given that I grew up in one of the hottest countries in the world. I do like my hot showers, my warm blanket or my partner in bed when it's cold. Who knows, maybe that is how my ice journey actually started, with the fire?

Somewhere top right is the field named after my fire

Chapter 5
Lesson in Survival

If you can sell encyclopaedias door to door, you can do anything, in my mind, anyway. Oddly enough, an ice mile was much more pleasant than cold-call knocking on doors in small mining towns in South Africa to sell encyclopaedias.

I was 23 years old, living in Johannesburg, I recovered well from my flirt with fire and I was in South Africa, getting ready to step into a job interview. Before I did, I contemplated where I had come from over the past few years; a captain in the Israeli army, a high school dropout, an avid windsurfer and a real upstart with an attitude. I knew how to command tanks, drive them, shoot any weapon and milk cows. But that didn't really add value to my CV.

It was 1981 and I was desperate to find a job. I had ended up in Johannesburg, chasing my first wife, Kim, whom I met in Israel at the kibbutz. Johannesburg, for whites, at that time, was a wonderful place. There was a high standard of living, high quality in everything and it was very intimidating to a young guy who had been very powerful a year before in the army. I was absolutely powerless there, in the jungle of Old South Africa.

Although I had started to develop some understanding of world politics and social structures, we still had no social media or instant communication of any sort. Newspapers, if you could trust them in those days, and radio were all we had to grow our knowledge of the world we lived in and outside of our borders. So, I had picked up an ad in the paper, which promised that I would make loads of money and didn't require any particular skill as the item pretty much sold itself. It sounded too good to be the truth, but I had no other options. On meeting Dave, a young guy with a strong cockney accent, I was asked one or two short questions. My English, at that time, was still rather basic and he plunged into a sales speech, which I had to focus on due to his strong dialect. He was very cheerful and charming, but I had no idea what he was saying. I just nodded and left 30 minutes later. The only thing I managed to get out of it was that I had been awarded the job and that the training started on Monday morning. I was ecstatic. I had a job. I had a purpose and I could stay in South Africa.

Johannesburg was a strange place in those days. Okay, it's a strange place these days too. But then everything was about black and white. Everything had a sign stating whether it was black or white property, domain or territory. I felt that all that I did was revolve around whether I was black or white too. I had to be very careful to follow the local rules and norms. Several times, I ended up, accidentally, on a bus or in a black liquor store. Racial and ethnic issues were not new to me. Israel had plenty and Israel had people from all over the world, all different cultures and skin colours. They all had one common thread, they were all Jews, but then Israel had Arabs as well, which complicated everything so much more.

I was used to religious divides, but such racial segregation was new to me and certainly confusing. My environment was mixed with white liberalism and the comfort of reality. I had decided to stay away from strong social, racial and political views. I certainly had and still have strong views on all subjects, but I also learnt how naïve we all are when we are young and how simple we see it all. Yet, I had already started to develop a strong humanitarian consciousness. I always believed everyone had the right to be treated with respect and be judged by their efforts and results rather than by prejudice, stereotypes and other limiting ideas. I learnt to judge people for who they were and what they were regardless of where they came from. What they looked like and what religion they believed in always brought on my healthy dose of sarcasm.

Anyway, Monday came and there I was sitting in a room, in a circle with a dozen other newbies, eager to start. Dave came in and began. We introduced ourselves and I quickly learnt that most were not South Africans. Some were from Rhodesia, the Zimbabwe of today and others from various English-speaking countries. They were tourists like me, but with no permit-seeking employment. There were only two non-native English, a Danish girl and myself.

A few weeks later, when we progressed to the streets and started working, the Danish girl cracked her first sale on her first night. It was a great lesson in survival, language, new environment and scary reality, but if you needed to survive, you could do magic!

The course was very structured. An American company and a group of Psychologists designed it. We were given a three-page sales speech. We had to memorise it and later on act on it, naturally, like a part in a film. I didn't understand half of what I memorised and in fact, six months down the line as a successful sales representative, I still didn't understand a few words, but I was good at acting them out. Luckily, my main client base was Afrikaans and I knew that many of them didn't understand half of what I said either. I didn't care really. If they bought the encyclopaedia and loved the idea of education, then I made a sale. The whole sales concept was based on 'buying education' rather than educating yourself. All you had to do was buy it and display it in your lounge. That was 90% of the education process. I would like to think that some actually used it once in a while but most just bought into the optics.

The course took us step by step from opening the door, to closing a deal. It was a hard week of sales technique education and it worked like magic. I did learn to hate it though over time, especially since it came down to blasting a client with structured bullshit. It fascinated me, however, how people just fell for it time after time. The trick was confidence and attitude. I got to know the encyclopaedia set quite well too, so I increased my general knowledge at the same time. It was good and it was highly ranked out there. If someone needed it, and many did, it was a good product. What I hated was the forced sales technique.

Later on, when we travelled through South Africa selling encyclopaedia door to door, we started every day with a few hours of training. The training was hard and unforgiving. We had no room for error or mistakes, else, no sales. Still, it was very hard. You ended up giving many presentations and sometimes closed a deal and most times not. If you spent a week not closing a deal, you were taken off the streets and had to join an experienced sales representative until you saw a deal closed next to you. It was done to rebuild your confidence, to show you that it could be done and people did buy these sets.

We were taught how to deal with various objections and rejections and how to turn them around into an opportunity. It wasn't hard for me as it was already somewhere in my nature. I just needed to be in the right state of mind to be able to deliver. Again, I realised how strong one's mind and mindset can be. If you got it right, you were invincible. If you didn't get it right, you were a miserable sod and no one would buy anything from you. Later in life, I learnt to run with this method to achieve the challenges I wanted to do. I realised that a strong mind with no passion and purpose behind it was empty and shallow. The course went by and we hit the road. The drill was simple.

Me with the Encyclopaedia sales kit at the end of the presentation

We had teams and the head of each team had a car and he or she was generally an experienced salesperson. They would take us around the country and would look after us. Petrol, accommodation and food were covered. All we had to do was sell, sell and sell. The head of the team would receive a commission on each of our sales, so if the team performed well, it was great money for him or her. To earn well as a sales representative, you had to be very good and sell lots of sets. People got burnt out very quickly and most didn't come back if they didn't make a sale whilst on the road trip. A road trip would be around ten days and would cover any remote location in South Africa. I ended up in most places in the country from Welkom to Klerksdorp, Kimberly to Phalaborwa and Ladysmith to Tenzin. I got to see South Africa inside out.

The routine was simple. The team leader took us to a location, usually a nice mining town, full of young families thirsty for education for their kids, who had a steady income and a very low cost of living. The Old South African middle class basically. We were each given three to four streets and were dropped at around 4 pm to be picked up at around 11 pm. We had seven hours on our own, in the streets and hopefully, mostly, inside people's houses selling. We always worked alone unless you accompanied someone to learn or later on taught someone how to crack a deal.

***

We would start by scanning the streets and getting to know the turf. I remember that some houses just looked perfect for a sale and some not. Some looked inviting and some hostile with a loud scary dog in the garden. It was amazing to see how much you could learn about a family just from looking at their house from the outside. Every little detail told a story. The family must have liked the house and modified it to their liking. This was critical to understanding your target. I used to look for interesting things around the house and use it as an icebreaker. (My early days of breaking the ice, lol!)

At around 5 pm, the first round started. I walked around door-to-door, making an appointment for later on once the family had settled in. To close a deal, you needed both husband and wife to be there. The deal had a seven-day cooling-off period and if you didn't have both of them, it had an almost 100% chance of defaulting. It was quite a significant amount of money, probably around two months' salary for a family like that and if the husband came back from work to find out his wife had bought a set of encyclopaedia for two months' salary, he would generally come to find you in the street and default the deal with you right there and then. That was not a pleasant option. These mining town guys came in XL or XXL sizes and as much as I hated this job at times, it taught me some real lessons in life.

Seven days of cooling off was a long time and all it took was a simple letter to cancel the deal. We had many sales reps that made many sales but had a

90% default rate. For me, it was another hard lesson in actual achievement versus a phantom one. I wasn't interested in glory or phantom achievements. I wasn't interested in being known for my phenomenal sales track record but rather for the size of the paycheque at the end of every month, however miniature it turned out to be. I focused on quality deals, closing deals and making sure my default rate was close to zero. That lesson still helps me a lot in any business I get involved in. The quality of deal and achievements sticks, but the bad quality of deal and achievement can haunt you for the rest of your life when you least expect it.

I learnt to spend two hours on the presentation and one hour on closing the deal. Even if the couple was eager to sign and paid the cash deposit, I always found some excuse to stick around longer. I felt that the deal needed to be properly cemented and to make sure that they had no dormant gremlins that would wake them up in the middle of the night with questions that may lead them to cancel the sale. It was that principle that I carried to my future businesses. If you think something can go wrong, anticipate it now!

At every door, I met the housewife with a very pleasant and polite manner. Entering the house was a big mistake. The appointment had to be done outside and at times, I had to be firm with this rule. If I came later and the wife told the husband about having tea with me whilst he was at work, that was the end of my sale. The appointment speech was around a survey that required both husband and wife.

At around 7 pm, after I managed to fill up my evening with appointments and a stop at the local café and a religious 20 minutes on the Pacman game, I started the sales round. I tried to pick the houses that created the impression of a possible sale, almost like a hobbit house but in a South African mining town. I prayed long and hard that the wife, and not the husband would answer the door. Not all husbands were accommodating to a young strange man with an accent at their door claiming to have made an earlier appointment with his wife while he was at work. That was when the real work started. The attitude was everything. Not cocky, not shy, not too professional and not, most certainly, lost. I used to hum *'Strangers in the Night'* by Frank Sinatra to get my attitude right and then the 'knock-knock' game started.

It took me a while to get my sales speech and process perfect, but once I got it right, it was amazing. The only thing that got in my way was confidence. We were told that once we knocked on the door, we had to take a step back, not too far, but make space for the person opening the door to see you and suss you out. We were told that the sale could be concluded in the first 15 seconds if you had the right approach and attitude. It was mostly correct. It still required two to three hours of hard sales work thereafter. The theory, like everything, was easy. But walking that theory was hard work.

Every door presented a new challenge, new personalities and a new approach. We had to adapt quickly and respond accordingly. It was then that I learnt that sales were not about bullshit, but about being good at what you did and to back your talk with action. Focus and know your facts. Bullshit would carry you a distance, but unless you were a master at that, it would fail. It was just a matter of time. I also learnt to understand my sales style and approach. I learnt what my strengths and weaknesses were in that field. But the most important thing I learnt was that you had to have a passion to succeed, real passion.

I met so many interesting families and learnt about their stories. My sales went very well and I even got my girlfriend at the time and future first wife and first ex-wife to sell those books. She did very well. It was an exhilarating period of hard work and hard play.

It was 1981 and the Lebanon war had just started. I found out about this somewhere in Sasolburg while selling a set to a family. They asked me about Lebanon. I had no idea. No news, no media, just travel, sales, party and fun. I asked around but couldn't get too much information. I learnt that Israel had invaded Lebanon and that there was a war going on. It was 1982. This war had always been on the verge of happening several times in my army career. I remember being flown from the Sinai Desert to the Lebanon border at 3 am a couple of times before. In the rain, freezing cold and mud, we took our tanks and headed to the border. It was an increasingly active border and it was a war waiting to happen.

So, on hearing something real had started, I called my mum in Israel and she played it down, a small incursion to Lebanon and not a war by Israeli standards. Later on, these 'small incursions' became a new reality. I called the Israeli embassy in South Africa to find out what was going on. I was a captain and whether I liked it or not, I knew I had to be there. The embassy played it down even more. Later, I realised that that was the media strategy in Israel. Keep it low-key to not attract too much attention. Well, I was having a good time and when I was told that no reserves were being called and it was just another border dispute, I carried on.

A few weeks later, I made it back to Cape Town, my new base in South Africa. I collected my mail and found a short letter from my mum. It didn't say much about the war, but it had a chilling list of my mates that had been killed in the war, all good officer friends and some ex-soldiers of mine. Lebanon's wars for tanks was hellish.

FUCK IT
I'm going home.

Time to go home

Later, the ongoing urban war in villages and Beirut brought other complicated hells to everyone. Lebanon was a mountainous beautiful country and once you left the coastline, it was all hills with narrow roads that hugged the landscape like snake coils between villages and little towns. That dictated a single file of tanks convoys with a mountain on one side and a cliff on the other side. Once you committed, you couldn't go back. You had to move forward to the next protected coil. Each tank would progress single file led by its captain, head sticking out, looking forward. The first tank would get hit first by snipers and as a tank captain, the odds were significantly against you.

That letter stuck in my mind for years and later when I went back, I found out that my reserve unit didn't go into Lebanon. It helped my guilty conscious a bit and it was then that I started to develop a serious loathing for wars, guns and everything related. I was never a pacifist. I understood the hard reality of living by the border and the need to protect your homeland, but the price paid was horrific. I am still blown away by the human need for unnecessary violence.

A couple of months later, the novelty of knocking on other people's doors in the dark, and offering them encyclopaedias faded completely. I realised it was time to go a get some real education and find a more interesting focus in life. That journey, chasing interests and challenges has never ended for me. It was time to go back home. I never knew, at that stage, that Cape Town in South Africa would become my home and my kid's home. I was 25 years old, a high school dropout, a tanks officer a door-to-door encyclopaedia salesman and rich in experiences.

Chapter 6
The Student – University Years

It was late 1982 and it was time to go back home and get some education. I had little money, but I did have some great new experiences and a major rank in the Israeli army.

I arrived at a very different Israel. The Lebanon war had changed it. I met with my friends and family, many lost someone and the entire country's mindset was 'post-Vietnam' like. No one was proud of what we had done, yet many had died for our country. It took me a few years to come to terms with the harsh reality of unnecessary wars, but that again is a hindsight point of view.

I ended up heading for Eilat, the Red Sea area, to look for a job. I wondered around and finally arrived at an interview in the best hotel in town. Five stars and there I was in flip-flops, shorts and unshaved applying for a security officer position. Luckily it was Israel, and my service credentials did the work. I did, however, have to shave, get a pair of proper shoes and some kind of a summer suit. I had to carry a gun and do my job. It was quite fun with lots of perks. I was mostly focused on guests stealing rather than any serious act of terrorism though. I spent a lot of time in the sun and the water and slowly started saving really slowly. It was around about the time they shot the movie *Sahara* in the nearby desert and I was offered a possible position as bodyguard to Brooke Shields. She was 17 years old at the time and needless to say, she was very pretty. But I just couldn't see myself doing it, well, possibly if they gave me a tank.

Over that time, I also learnt an interesting lesson about the stock market. It was apparently a bull market and everyone was punting the stock market. I had no idea what was going on, but everyone, including the lifesaver, the barman and the receptionist were talking about the stock market, so I figured I had to get involved. It was crazy. I just bought what everyone else was punting and it lasted for around two months. I remember a few days when the 'profit' on my share portfolio was more than my monthly salary.

It was such fun, but then one day, the shares fell 50%, the next day 17% and the next day another 10% and my share portfolio got decimated. It was so surreal to lose everything in just a few days. But in truth, it was never mine. I never realised it or used it, nevertheless, it was much like watching a thriller. I did lose most of what I saved in my six-month stint in the Red Sea. Unfortunately, it wasn't a great movie I was watching.

The one good thing I learnt was that I was not a great gambler. And it stayed with me for life. I made a decision that day. I wouldn't get into risks I didn't understand. I would always need to understand my odds. Well, okay, I didn't calculate my risk very well when it came to my two divorces, but they were not really about risk, they were about love and…

I decided it was time to get a real education and despite everyone trying to convince me to get some night courses or some skills, I decided to go all the way and go do a degree in math and physics. I had a minor problem though; I was a high school dropout. So, I started investigating the various options I had in Israel. They all required good matric results in both maths and science. So, I decided to pay a visit to my old high school. Both the teacher that had expelled me and that same chemistry teacher that I had never liked were running the school. It felt like walking into a minefield with my eyes wide open.

But I had a plan. I needed to get into a course that replaced matric. It was a six-month intensive course in maths, physics, chemistry and English. If I got good marks, I would get into that university for the maths/physics major. I did, however, need to prove that I had finished high school. I explained my plans to the high school head and thought he would be delighted that the rebel was finally making a decision to get some education. But it wasn't as easy as that.

After some negotiation, they agreed to give me a letter that stated that I spent the years 1971 to 1974 in that high school. It didn't say that I finished high school though. All it said was that I was present there from 1971 to 1974 equating to four years. It didn't say that I joined at the end of 1971 and was kicked out at beginning of 1974.

Nevertheless, that letter worked and I managed to enrol in the course. I was very rusty when it came to maths and physics and I had a minor problem, no money. I was 26 years old.

I quickly looked around and managed to get a fun job as an undercover officer checking for smuggled fruits and vegetables from various farms around Israel. I was given a hired car, a police radio and there I went. I called one of my mates and he joined me as my partner. We had no idea how to go about it and what to do, but the salary was great. We had loads of freedom and fun. It could have gotten quite serious and we were warned to tread carefully when we visit the lords of the fruit's underworld. We had the authority to stop and confiscate illegal fruit transportation. But the guys were much smarter than us and we ended up knowing what was going on but not really getting involved.

I was saving for the university not chasing Al Capone. We had a few intense moments. We visited some dodgy places around the country, but we also had lots of fun. We changed our car every two weeks trying different models, different types, under the excuse that we were undercover and needed a different car, or else they would start to recognise us. It worked. I traversed the country every day, met many people and learnt a lot. I think that my mindset, post-Lebanon war and the atmosphere in Israel, helped me to stay out of trouble, for a change.

Apparently, our presence made some impact and the co-op was happy with our progress. They clearly knew that we were there for visibility with no skills to take down the fruits mafia in Israel. What fascinated me was the fact that I was never offered a bribe.

A week after I left, my partner was assigned with an old fox partner that has been doing this for 20 years. He told me that they were offered stuff all the time. All his partner did was park the car open at some places in the fruit and vegetable market to drive home and find the boot full of fruits, eggs and vegetables. I am still hurt that no one ever offered me a bribe.

Anyway, it was time to go back to school. What a shock! Ten years after high school, plunging straight into matric level maths and physics. I was way out of my comfort zone, but luckily, there were a few of us and two kids aged 16 years old, who were kicked out of high school for being too bright. They had a little calculator that could do square equations and similar things. That was pure science fiction for me.

The course went fast and I dived into the deep. After a bit, I was called back to the army for three weeks exactly at final exam time. It was a reality, not a disaster. I simply had to adapt or give up. I managed to write my exams a few weeks after the end of the course alone in a room. The benefits there were that I had no real pressure or time limit, which suited me fine. It was over; I passed and got accepted to university.

The summer holiday was disappearing and then the first year of university came. This university offered pure maths and physics, but it was structured to qualify teachers, so one day a week, we had to spend a half-day in 'group dynamic' exercise and the second half was psychology. The psychology part was easy. I simply sat down and did my physics and maths projects. I didn't care much for my marks and knew it was something I had to do to pass. However, group exercises were completely different. I had to participate. I had to contribute and show interest, which I had, honestly, none. I had come here to study maths and physics, period.

When I was challenged about my severe lack of interaction, I made my position clear, "I'm not interested, please leave me alone and I promise not to interfere." That, of course, created a great challenge for my tutors and they decided that winning me over was their mission for the year. Needless to say, they lost, but not without a hard battle. I managed to get into trouble in just about every discussion. By the time I was forced to interact and state my thoughts about the topic, I was quite irritated and boy, I did state my thoughts clearly. That changed the dynamics of the discussions from boring and stale to fun and exciting.

I usually came out bruised at the end of the process, but the tutors realised they had a gold mine in me. Every time the discussions fell quiet with no participation, they forced me to get involved. I actually walked out a few times knowing what was going to follow. But most of the time they managed to get the spark that started the fire.

I clearly remember one session when we all sat in a circle and had various drawings that some of the students produced, all laid down on the floor in the middle of the group. We were tasked to go out for 10 minutes and come back with an item that would symbolise our thoughts and place it on the drawings in a place where we wanted to state our opinion.

Great task. I needed a smoke break anyway. I went out and realised I was still tired from working most of the night. I needed coffee and quietness, so I lit my cigarette, looked down and saw gravel. I picked up a small stone and when I went back in, I sat down, leaned forward reached the drawings and placed it on the nearest edge of the drawings closest to me. It took around five minutes and the discussion was stale again. The tutor suddenly spotted the stone that was quietly resting on the edge of the drawings. He asked who had placed it there. I couldn't hide, so I admitted guilt.

He asked me to explain the symbolism of the stone in the corner, almost off the drawings. I explained exactly what happened, hoping to be left alone and allow for the deep discussion to continue its course. It never happened. I happened to insult someone who took my action very personally regardless of my trying to dig myself out of this hole. I learnt a lot about honesty and bullshit in that course. I learnt that most people when asking you for your honest opinion, want to hear exactly what they think and hope you are going to be polite rather than tell them your actual honest opinion. I also learnt that many people are very happy to spend their time having inane conversations. Life is hard enough to be constantly reminded of its harshness. Another lesson I learnt well but still struggle to execute.

Regardless, the first year was amazing. I loved maths and physics, but I was struggling a lot and was at the bottom of the class. I did, however, manage to recover and finished around the top. I loved the theory of science and the purity of maths and physics.

Of those two gifted kids, one had to leave and follow his family overseas, his dad, a physics professor who was transferred to Canada. I decided to adopt the other kid and he became my study partner and I became his mentor. I told him about my army and life and he helped me with the math. He was a clearly gifted genius and sadly, I have no idea what happened to him later. He used to correct our professors' charting proofs from their notes on the blackboard. They simply made a mistake copying stuff from their notes. He would follow intensely and then say, "Sorry, sir, but that equation doesn't make sense." The professor would look at his notes, see what it was and correct them. They knew the kid and they never challenged him. His paper reminded me of the stories I had heard about Mozart. He used to write his operas straight on his music notes, with no mistakes and no corrections, like a brain dump right onto the notes.

The highlight of the first year was my little dog. I used to drive a small Vespa to university and I woke up one morning to go to leave when I heard a faint whimper. There, on the street was a little three-week-old pup. It was a mixed breed of Labrador and something smaller. I didn't know what to do, so I picked it up, and knocked on all the doors around but no luck. I wasn't ready for this but went back home, spread a few newspapers on the floor, set a little bowl of water and milk down and rushed to university.

When I came back in the afternoon, my flat was redecorated completely. The newspapers were thoroughly read and dissected into millions of pieces all over the place. They were also covered with stuff that I never knew could come out of such a little cute fluffy thing. The smell stayed in my flat until the day I left, but I had no choice. I was hopelessly in love. I named the little creature Infi (pronounced 'infy') taken from my math course infinitesimal mathematics. That little thing started studying maths and physics with me, visiting restaurants, going into banks and basically took over my life.

At that stage of my life, I had developed another great passion and love of windsurfing. The year went by quickly and I found myself discovering computers. I did some work on the first apple computer in our lab and I was fascinated. It was time to move further. I couldn't handle the teaching aspect of my course. I realised I would always be a useless teacher as I simply didn't have the patience for it.

I started shopping around for another university. I was looking for a math and/or physics major still. It so happened that the dean of the Haifa math faculty was a close relative of my family. He was very honest with me and despite the fact that he was one of the leading researchers in his field, maths, in the world, his words were, 'There are around 5 people around the world who really understand what I do.'

He pointed out how competitive the world of maths was. He also pointed out that 95% of his students may be extremely bright but only 5% ended up doing something meaningful with their gift. Haifa University was the best one in Israel when it came to maths. Tel Aviv was physics and the Technicon was computer science, so I went to visit Tel Aviv University.

In the future class of the next year, there were two 13-year-old 'students' who walked around holding their mother's hand. They were going for a double major in maths and physics. I had a real wake-up call. There I was 27 years old. I knew I wasn't stupid, but I also realised that I would always be a minor player in the field. It was the usual debate between passion and competence. Mozart vs. Salieri. I was no Mozart, that I knew. I decided to follow competence and went to do computer science. As much as I loved maths, I didn't regret that. I have used it a lot in my working career, but I was also passionate about computers. A combo of a nerdy rebel but also an adventurous beach bum. The Technicon University produces many of the technological wiz-kids who populate Israel.

Many start-ups and Nasdaq-listed companies were the brainchild of this university.

I worked hard. It wasn't an easy four-year journey, but I met many extremely gifted people and many more just hard-working students who, with their tenacity, ended up with PhDs. I learnt about the balance between natural raw talent and real grit, perseverance and commitment. I realised that a good combo of perseverance with the right amount of passion can take you very far. None of them led to much on its own. But the right combo could take you to unimaginable places.

Practising Karate

Sadly, I had to let go of my little Infi. I gave her to one of my best friends with a promise that I have the first option on her first litter. I exercised this option two years later when the first of the litter arrived. I chose the spicy red-headed little thing and named her Mariko. I was very much into martial arts and karate in those days, reading a lot about Japan. Mariko sounded like the right name. Mariko ended up graduating with me in computer science. She burnt the midnight oil in the computer centre with me and marked every part of the territory there.

Much happened with romance and the softer part of life at that time, which led to my first marriage, three of my four amazing kids and my first divorce. But that stays with me.

My windsurfing passion took serious priority and I ended up spending most of my weekends in the water chasing the wind. The wind had become an obsession for us too. We spoke about the wind all the time. When we surfed, it was 100%, nothing less. I had a very tight group of friends all suffering from the same addiction to the wind. When the wind blew, we simply dropped everything and ran.

The summer wind was a thermal wind that picked up almost daily as the temperature differences between the ground and the sea reached a point and created a thermal wind. When this wind started, I could see it approaching from the window in my lecture room. Sometimes, when the wind looked exceptionally strong and inviting, I used to bunk lectures get on the next bus home and manage to catch a few hours of windsurfing, later heading back to the university on the 6 am bus.

I found that this combination of physical and mental stimulation worked very well for me. I always liked that connection between the body and the mind. Still today, I get grumpy if that alignment is not right. As I got older, the physical element took precedence since my health became more and more important to me. Those days, we were simply invincible. We studied hard, partied hard, windsurfed hard and somehow managed to chill as well. To date, when I see youth on the go, I say, "Don't hold back, ride that wave and max it." I fully believe in following my passions. It may never be so easy as those days, yet, it never stops, just changes form and priorities.

I also had to find time to work. Money was not readily available and I had to find ways to fund my life, my study and my passions. I spent the last year in varsity working almost a full-time job, writing accounting software for a large factory, tutoring maths and teaching Lotus 1-2-3. I also learnt a lot about my strengths and weaknesses. Some courses were simply incomprehensible and some were a walk in the park. They were not divided into easy subjects or hard subjects. It was an interesting discovery as to how my brain worked. Some seemingly very difficult topics were exciting and easy for me and some, like economics, were like a big wall I had to climb just to get to the other side.

The end was approaching for my studies and if I had any regrets, it would be that I didn't stick around to progress my studies for a few more years, but at that stage, I was 30 years old with huge debt and with no idea how I would ever pay it back. But mostly, I had a huge desire to start living again. Romance and love had caused havoc in my life at the time and I finally decided to head towards Japan. I found a home for my little Mariko and I swore I would never have a dog again if I couldn't keep it forever.

Me and my dogs in later years – Bonnie and Clyde

I broke this promise with my second divorce. My German Shepard's Bonnie and Clyde, brother and sister, left with my ex-wife Nadine. But it was the right decision for my dogs although it broke my heart again.

Anyway, I finished all my courses. I walked to the registrar's office and picked up a document that stated that I had graduated and had accumulated the required amount of points. All done!

So, I did two things. I went to my best mate at the time and asked him to pick up my certificate at the graduation ceremony. Next, I went to a travel agent and bought a one-way ticket to Japan.

Chapter 7
The Passion of Windsurfing

8 days a week nearly cost me my university

It is simply impossible to describe what water and wind together meant to me. It was pure, wet, fast and challenging.

It was the summer holiday during university days. I was working during the day and windsurfing in the afternoons.

I worked mostly at the windsurfing club at the kibbutz holiday resort. I was running the club with a few friends, renting kayaks and giving windsurfing lessons. It was fun and hard work dealing with demanding holidaymakers, but it was on the beach, in the water. It was tough. The real day started in the late afternoon with the wind, we so worshipped those days.

The combination of wind, water and speed, all-natural, and no motors were as good as it gets. The wind was pumping and we were screaming across the waves into the deep. It was Friday afternoon. Summer, hot and like every afternoon, 3 pm, the wind came rolling down the hills into the sea of Galilei. I was surfing with Jeremy and Omri, some of my old best mates, as mad as me when it came to the sea and the wind. We were on our own tiny custom boards. We design them and dictated every aspect, but we got someone pro to build them for us. We spent all our savings at the time to build this magic windsurfing board. Mine was a skinny short purple 'sinker', which I named 'crazy diamond'. A combo of Pink Floyd influence and the fact that Dimond Head in Hawaii was at the time the Mecca of all windsurfers around the world. Jeremy had a pink board, I think he named it 'frog', after…maybe a frog, he kissed once. Both were super sinkers, and high wind speed machines.

A sinker is a board that requires a water start. It is too thin and short to stand on it, it basically sinks a foot underwater. However, any strong windsurfer with some self-respect at that time had to have a sinker. The more radical the board, the more radical and harder core you were. It did come with several complications; it needed strong wind, at least 15 knots else it would…sink! And swimming, dragging a board attached to a four-square metre sail is not easy.

We traversed the Sea of Galilee as if we owned it. It's a big lake called the sea, 22 km by 10 km, freshwater fed mostly from the Jordan river, which collects snowmelt and rain from the Golan Heights and the Lebanon mountains and it drains at the south into the Jordan River all the way to the dead sea, if they let water out.

We felt very safe in this large lake although the wind was pumping at 30–35 knots raising small chop and waves. Every now and then a 'big' wave would form, one to one and a half metres and we would try our best to get airborne. It was just heaven. The air temperature was close to 30°C, we were in swimming shorts and it was around 3 pm. We sailed up and down for hours far into the lake until the sun was starting to head down. What we forgot in this euphoric session is that as the sun comes down, the thermodynamics of the lake changes and the wind drops quite fast.

I was with Jeremy, it was close to 8 pm, we were around 4 km from the nearest shore when the wind suddenly dropped. On a sinker, you don't need a significant drop to start sinking. Jeremy was around 200 m on my side as we both realised we are sinking with the board and the wind has simply died to a standstill. The sea was still rough and lumpy and I still have that picture burnt in my mind of Jeremy and me sinking on our boards, shouting to each other to stay together and head with the waves to the nearest shore, Kibbutz Ein Gev. That was the last time I saw Jeremy in the water. We settled down for a long swim dragging a board with a large sail on the water behind us. We kept shouting at each other for a while and when no answer came back it was quite eerie. The sun was gone and the darkness settled in. Strange enough, I wasn't scared but I was tired and I was worried about Jeremy.

I could see in the distance the lights on the shore and push. Every now and then I would get on the board and paddle with the sail held up with my legs. Needless to say, it was very tiring. I made very slow progress, swimming with my right arm and doing breaststroke kicking while my left arm hanging on the board. The thought of leaving the board never crossed my mind. It was a precious windsurfer and it was safer to spend the night at sea on top of the board. I was getting tired and a little cold, more fatigue cold than actually cold. We were windsurfing for around five hours before the wind died. It was pitch dark and all I could do was swim. I grew up in this water, I knew every part of the lake, but I didn't have much experience in the dark alone and I had no idea how long I am going to be there. Luckily, the lake was clean freshwater, so every now and then I would stop, drink a gallon or two and carry on. Those days we knew nothing about nutrition, feeding every 30 minutes, electrolytes, carbs, sugar and the rest. We just went out on pure energy, excitement a cigarette and a few beers for hours and hours.

The water plays mind games with you in the dark. Especially with small waves all around. You hear things, you see things and you feel things. The only thing that could scare me in this lake was the giant catfish or barbel. They were black, slimy and moved like an eel. Some of them could have been larger than me. They were harmless but if something larger than you, slimy and fast brushes at you in the middle of the sea in the dark, you are bound to get several heart attacks. The wave tips also play on your mind, reflecting in the moonlight and many times look like a fast-travelling fin. I was safe as long as I stayed afloat, but still, every now and then my mind was testing me.

Every open water, marathon swimmer knows that at some stage, time and space fold into a place where time stops and flies at the same time. I knew I am covering distance, possibly more with the wave than my kicking, which was always useless. I kept on correcting towards the brightest lights on the shore, but I had no idea if I was going in the right direction. I didn't care, I needed land with lights, people, safety and most importantly, food! I was getting really hungry. I've been in the water for several hours spending energy with nothing to take in. I didn't have a watch, so I had no idea what the time was and how long I have been there. It was late in the evening, I started to smell food being cooked, eaten and appreciated. I focused on that smell and moved towards it. I kept on swimming and I started visualising the food. Trying to analyse the smell and decompound it to its ingredients. Meat? Roast chicken? Toast? Vegetable stew? I could smell it all and I started eating it carefully with my mind, appreciating it.

I started to hear sounds, and people's voices and I knew I am close. But in the dark and the sea, sounds carried far and I had no idea how far. I was worried about Jeremy. I had no idea if he was okay? I assumed he was, but I lost him very early and I couldn't understand why we would drift apart so quickly. You can swallow some water or cramp and lose it. You can get stuck under the big sail if a little gust of wind throws it over you. Things can go wrong and they have gone wrong many times before, I was worried, but there was nothing I could do aside from continue swimming, dragging the windsurfer flat on the water behind me.

I was very close; I could feel it. I started to see windows with lights and silhouettes of people, I was almost there. I felt the ground underneath my feet. I arrived. I dragged the windsurf with me and found a safe place to park it. I walked around in wet shorts, very tired, wearing a windsurfing harness. I asked someone what the time was, it was 11:30 pm. So, I was in the water swimming for close to four hours. I asked where I was and it was Kibbutz Ein Gev. I knew the windsurfing crowd there and asked for their place. I managed to find one of them in his room. He told me, to my relief, that Jeremy was there ten minutes ago and he was heading back home with a lift and looking for me. Remember, no cell phones those days. Communication was done personally face to face. I managed to get a lift back home with my windsurfer, connected with Jeremy and we both looked for food. Jeremy was fine, a little concerned but, like me, he wasn't really scared, just another very long day in the sea.

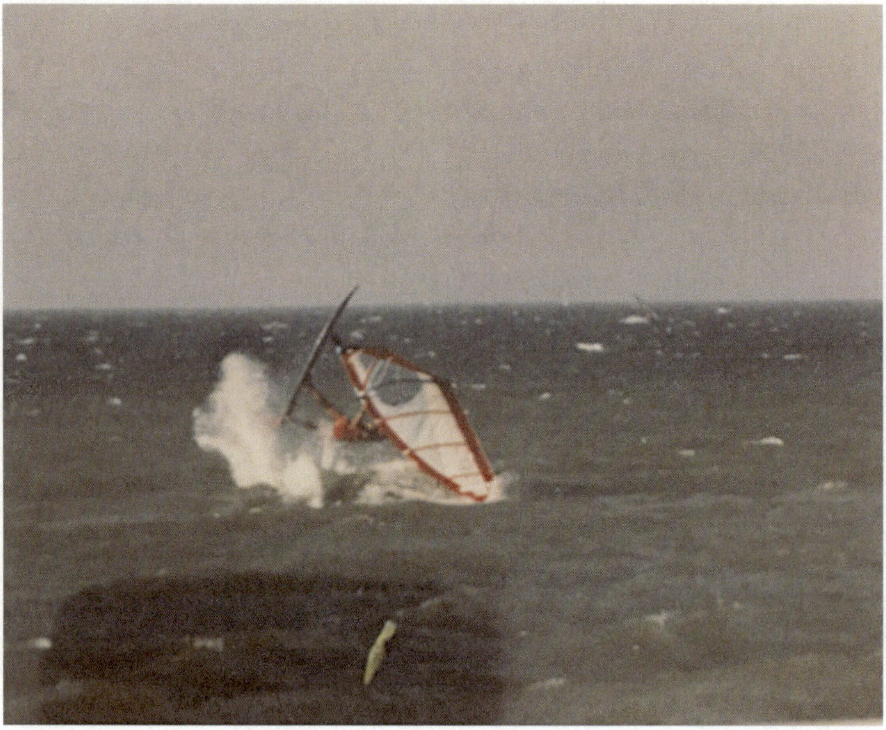

Chapter 8
Tokyo and Sushi

I finished university with a one-way ticket to Tokyo. I arrived at Tokyo, Narita Airport on Christmas Eve, 1987. I had $1000 cash in my bag, $14,000 debt in student loans and a backpack. As a 30-year-old retired major of the Israeli army with a degree in computer science under my belt, Tokyo seemed like a good enough place to escape to and since I had just broken off with my then-girlfriend/future wife-to-be, the idea was brilliant.

A few months earlier to my hasty departure, Tokyo had been in the middle of a global financial crisis. I had no idea and it was only years later, working for Flemings in Tokyo, that I read the book about Nomura Bank, realising that just across the desk, the ex-head of Nomura sales desk was sitting there next to me in Flemings.

Tokyo was as alien to me as Mars. Every sign in English, which were very few, referred to us *Gaijins* (non-Japanese or foreigners) as aliens. I had never seen this before. I knew I was a tourist or at least a foreigner, but I hadn't considered myself an alien.

I spent three hours at the airport trying to find a place to stay. My older brother, Hemi, was there somewhere with his new girlfriend selling pictures. I intended to link up with him at some stage. I had no intention of looking for a job as I was just there to clear my mind, take part in some martial arts and have fun. I quickly realised that Tokyo, being the most expensive city in the world, would eat up my $1000 before I could even start scouring the job ads.

I finally managed to find a place in a remote guest house called Mickey House. They had a bed and it was manageable. It was also only 30 minutes off from Ikebukuro Station on the Yamamoto line, which surrounds inner Tokyo city. Still today, I have no idea how I found the place. All train station signs were in Japanese. Announcements were in Japanese, and I quickly realised the Japanese don't speak English at all! I found out that it wasn't because they didn't want to, it was purely a mental thing or a saving face issue. They would not speak English unless they were perfect at it. Later, teaching English to Japanese kids, businessmen and others for six months, I enforced that phenomenon, making sure the Japanese would struggle with English for a few more generations.

Selling pictures in the streets of Tokyo with Hemi

So, remember, it was 1987 i.e., no cell phones, no public phones and no google map only paper maps, no Airbnb and no WhatsApp, nothing like we have today! All I had was my survival instincts and they were razor sharp. I knew I could disappear in Tokyo to be never found again if I chose to get lost there. Around 20 million people moved around Tokyo during the day. At night, most of them were so drunk, that it was like a scene from the *Walking Dead* series. Needless to say, months later, I found myself walking with the 'dead', breathing fumes that could easily torch the ice wall in the *Games of Thrones*.

You know how it goes…when in Rome…

One of my survival tactics was to memorise the names of the stations. With Japanese being a phonetic language, this made my job easier. I, somehow, managed to move from one train line to another and finally found myself at the final station, in a little suburb, on the outskirts of Tokyo. It was very quaint with small wooden houses everywhere. It had been a very long day; it was dark and cold by the time I got there and it was Christmas Eve…on Mars. I traversed the little alleys for an hour and finally found Mickey House. I opened the sliding door and walked in, kicking my shoes off. I was saved! The room was filled with English-speaking people from all over the world. I could understand and communicate! What a relief!

After being shown a bunk bed, I dropped my stuff and was offered a drink. As the evening descended, more and more people came in from their various work locations around Tokyo. Christmas it was and although I am Jewish, I am pretty much non-religious. That Christmas party was a god gift to me.

I woke up in the lounge, with few others, at 11 am, my first morning in Tokyo with a severe hangover, the first one but certainly not the last one. The Japanese love their drink after work, but they are not very good at holding it down, which gave us, the aliens, a massive competitive advantage.

The next few days, followed by a New Year's Eve party, somewhere at another remote guest house, went by in a thick cloud of alcohol. It wasn't my fault, your honour! I was forced by everyone to join in. It was just what everyone did that time of the year. The guest house was, again, full of 'aliens' from all over the world. Most were English speaking because teaching English to Japanese was in huge demand, well paid and required no qualifications. They also loved the North American accent and stories. Many were just like me, moving through Japan away from some unresolved issues at home and feeling safe on Mars. Tokyo is so big that you can live there for 20 years and disappear one day with no one noticing.

But I also went to Japan because I was attracted to its oriental mystique, hence I named my dog Mariko and I studied karate. Eventually, I managed to find my brother, Hemi, and we ended up selling pictures to drunken Japanese men outside bars in the red-light districts. Negotiating on dark corners with the local Yakuza (Japanese mafia) and sometimes ending up drinking with them was par for the course. As long as we didn't interfere and remain *gaijins*, we were safe. It was fun and fascinating, but I hated it. Standing on street corners late at night, freezing to death, waiting for the guys to come out of the bars, on route home, to sell a few plastic-framed pictures of Michael Jackson or Tom Cruise. I have no idea what they did with those pictures, but we, the aliens, exploited their culture and their inability to say no. It was rude to refuse our effort in offering them a Michael Jackson picture, which, by the way, only cost us a few cents and we sold it at $10 to $20.

The best part was spending some late nights with my brother in remote locations in bigger Tokyo. We made enough to cover our costs. Selling pictures in the streets of Tokyo was an Israeli-run endeavour and soon many others joined in. It was hard and unpleasant work, but it was certainly character-building and allowed us to see interesting parts of Japan and the Japanese culture.

I survived for a few weeks hating every minute and then one day when I got back to Mickey House, I heard a few guys from Pakistan saying that they were teaching English. They certainly didn't have the Californian look, nor could they speak English well enough to teach, but they did all the same. So, just like many other challenges in my life, I got some perspective and realised it was possible.

After I had called around for interviews, I started compiling an honest CV. My English was good enough and stating that my accent was 'South African' was a good thing. In those days, South Africans were not allowed in Japan, so everyone fell for it. But very quickly, I realised I needed to polish up my CV and I changed my history, slightly. My Israeli background parents from Transylvania, tanks and being an army officer was not an advantage. So, I swapped my life with a born South African, who went to the army in Israel and studied there. It explained a few things, including my accent. Luckily, the Japanese I thought could barely speak English, so I happily contributed to their ignorance and made sure that the status quo remained.

To be honest, most of them didn't really care. They would have paid good money just to spend an hour with a foreigner. They had never been exposed to one before and the experience was fascinating for them. We used to call ourselves monkeys because we felt like it, but it was a mutually beneficial relationship and both sides knew it.

I landed a job in a proper English school. The owner, a Chinese lady, married to a Canadian guy, really liked me and had her partner/owner, Howard, from Dublin, call me to extend his congratulations. I received the call while I was at Mickey House and he offered me a job…I think. It was my first encounter with a thick Irish accent, which years later, I learnt to love and understand a little more. I realised he was speaking English and when he suddenly asked me, "Ram, are you a native English because your accent is a little odd…"

I shot back, "Are you? Your accent is a little odd as well." I got the job, but then I had serious ethical issues. I couldn't sleep all night. I knew I couldn't take the job on a lie, so I decided to go and meet Howard and tell him the truth.

I travel to school the next day and met him. I told him the truth and I declined the offer. He was a very good man. He listened to me and said that he had known I wasn't being truthful but couldn't be 100% sure. Howard said Lee, the other owner, really liked me and as long as I kept it to myself, he was happy to take me on still. Lee couldn't tell the difference and I had a real job. My love affair with the Irish accent continues to date, but I still struggle to understand them after a few drinks.

Later, I met a bunch of them, engineers, working in Tokyo during the day and playing in and around Tokyo at night. Surprisingly, two out of the five were Sean. Little Sean from Dublin, who stayed at the same block of flats with U2, when they were just a small band and Big Sean from Belfast, who played the bass guitar.

With my English teaching team in Tokyo

I decided to go to Waseda University in Tokyo to see the karate club. My Karate style *Sense*, or teacher, was from this university. I studied Shotokan and very hard and rigid form of karate, mostly linear, pure and lethal if you can master it. Waseda and Tokyo universities were the two top universities in Tokyo and Japan as a country. I went to visit and found two aliens training there, American and Israeli, both senior black belts. To be accepted, you had to be introduced and vouched for. In addition, it was free and very prestige. I got in and started training.

For the Japanese students, it was just a sport. For us, it was art. I started training three hours a day, deep in Japanese culture. I was accepted as long as I followed their rules and rituals to the tee and did not try to be Japanese. It was a lesson I learnt later on; don't pretend to be Japanese, just because you think you 'are in'. You are never in! You always will be *gaijin* and as long as you stay one, you are accepted and can get away with anything.

Karate in Japan was also giving me a unique window into their culture. I ended up training at their global main *Dojo*, a training place, with people from all over the world. Many black belts travelled to Japan to receive their second black belt in Tokyo. It was an experience mixed with prestige. I truly enjoyed it despite the fact that during those few years I have tested the resilience of many of my bones. I broke my ribs around 6 times, my nose three times and a few fingers. All are well and strong. It gave me a lot of confidence although I am as rust as the scarecrow in the wizard of Oz, nowadays.

Even fourth-generation *gaijin*s born in Japan were not eligible for citizenship. Things may have changed since then though. I just loved it. It was a hard routine, but I got stronger and better every day. It is an experience very few *gaijin*s are exposed to. My Israeli friend was working as an engineer for Toshiba and he asked me why didn't I look to join him in on the computer game. To be honest, it had never crossed my mind. I was an alien on Mars. It was as simple as that.

That day, I went to the stationery store and bought a pack of CVs. In Japan, everything has a formal standard form and it has to be completed by hand. I also bought a thick job classified booklet, in Japanese of course, and started scanning it for something familiar. Computer jobs use a lot of technical terminologies, so when I saw the letter C or C++ or Unix, I knew it was what I studied and took down the address. I was set. With a dictionary in hand, I studied the short questions in the CV form. After filling it up, in English, I sent 20 CVs to the Tokyo computer companies.

I had to copy the address in Japanese onto the envelopes and it took me many hours to get the Japanese characters just right. The Japanese have three sets of alphabets, Katakana, with 26 phonetic characters. Katakana is used for foreign words that don't exist in the Japanese language. Hiragana is used as 'easy' Japanese and to connect the Chinese characters, the Kanji is used, which is the main set of characters and there are thousands of them. You need to know around 1800 of them to read the newspaper and 2000 for university. I knew around 100 when I left and have forgotten all of them since.

The next day, I received a phone call and I was invited for an interview. It was such a relief to be able to simply tell the truth about my background and qualifications, which I was proud of. The firm was a Japanese software firm, I. Brains. I was the first-ever *gaijin* to be employed there. Every morning at 9 am, we used to stand in a circle, the seniors would greet everyone good morning and off we would go to our desks. I sat next to Shibata san, who had a degree in English Literature but could barely string a sentence together. I was relieved. It wasn't entirely my fault the nation couldn't speak English.

Every Monday, one of us had to tell a short story about their weekend before we went to our desks. I was told my turn would be up after three months. I spent the entire night before my turn sitting with Little Sean, who had a Japanese girlfriend, with a few beers and he helped me to write a one-pager about my weekend. I was a nervous wreck that morning. I read that story in Japanese or what I thought sounded like Japanese. There was no applause and no congratulations. It was not their culture to react that way, so everyone just went to their desk afterwards. It was like that every Monday. I sat down and leaned over to Shibata-san asking her how I had done, and did she understand it. She replied it was very good and that she understood nothing, but well done, Barkai-san. Oh, well!

I could write books about my time in Japan. It was a mind-blowing experience. There was that time when I was given a top-end Omron Unix workstation as a computer and an Intel 8069 microchip manual. I was told to write a software simulator that would mimic that chip 100%. It took me six months before I was done and I had very little help from anyone. I simply had to figure it all out by myself, another character-building exercise.

I did make friends and one was from the Israeli University. We met on the subway and Taschi was his name. I helped find him a job in computers as well and we became good friends, sharing our frustration with *gaijins* working in Japan.

Life in Tokyo was good. I started to get a real salary, moved into an apartment with some mates and started to feel 'at home'. I had to study Japanese for my work visa and it still comes back to me when I meet a Japanese and have had a few beers to help lubricates my tongue. Eventually, my visa ran out and I had to leave the country to apply for a long-term working visa. At that stage, I renewed contact with my ex-girlfriend, Kim, and planned to go see her in Cape Town. It was early 1989 and I had been in Japan by that stage for around 18 months. It was home.

Waiting for sunrise on top of Mount Fuji, Japan

I arrived in Cape Town, applied for my working visa and continued to consult my Japanese firm from the beach. The windsurfing was good and I got back together with Kim, a wedding was on the horizon. The wedding took place in the church her parents got married in, but the minister was kind enough to allow me to break a glass as per the Jewish tradition and insisted on sharing with me his wonderful experience of Israel and Herzliya golf course.

We got married in January 1990 and left soon after that to get back to Tokyo, it was the day Nelson Mandela was released from jail. Unfortunately, no one bothered to inform us of his release early enough. Tickets were booked and a honeymoon was paid for in Thailand, Singapore and Tokyo.

My old boss had left the company and offered me the opportunity to join him in his start-up. I had options and I managed to negotiate a better package. By then, I was driving an old Suzuki 250cc, which a friend had left for me and we found a little Japanese wooden house outside Tokyo in Ogikubo, 15 minutes from work. The house was a typical Japanese house, wooden with tatami mat floors, sliding doors and windows. Our bedroom was half a meter from the next-door neighbour's bedroom and once a month their kids went to stay with the grandparents and then we didn't sleep all night…our own live entertainment.

By that stage, I felt fairly at home in Japan. I had a real job and I was doing martial arts regularly. Kim managed to find a job teaching English and for the first time, I started to feel like a real grown although I was the tender age of 32 by then. Life was very surreal. It was Tokyo, Japan, we were still very much aliens, but I suppose we adapted. We used to go to the same restaurants and bars all the *gaijin*s went to, so we could speak English and share our experiences and loneliness on this planet.

There were several bars where all the *gaijin*s who were married to Japanese used to go to. My boss would drag me around to meet all his Japanese colleagues, many well-known, but none of them spoke English. It was exhausting and frustrating. My limited Japanese allowed me to understand a little but not to converse. Being a *gaijin*, I felt, again, like the circus monkey on display. Most conversations were bloated with nervous laughter, miscommunication and headaches. Once alcohol, the blessed social lubricator, was introduced, things changed dramatically.

The Japanese society was so structured by rituals and codes of conduct that you never really saw their real personality, well, only after the alcohol. When the alcohol was introduced, their personality erupted like a volcano and covered you with way too much information about their personal lives, experiences, and fantasies. Suddenly English emerged from the volcanic ashes and you were bombarded by questions. I got used to it, but never really felt at ease. The Japanese appreciated *gaijin*s that got seriously intoxicated and played the game. Unfortunately, my personality and individuality weren't very welcome there. Adults were expected to fit in and adhere to the complex social system that underlined Japan. I clearly was a misfit, again!

Understanding the rich Japanese history would help one understand their culture. General McCarthy undid centuries of family-controlled culture, but below the surface, the culture is still very traditional and many times invisible to the foreign eye.

The work in a small Japanese start-up was a real challenge. I was handed a big manual in Japanese and was asked to write a complex system. Luckily, some technical text was in English with few design specs. I ended up in a huge national project that covered most big IT companies in Japan. As fascinating and challenging as it was, it drained me to sit in technical meetings with dozens of engineers and programmers all in Japanese, of course. I was amazed at how much I could actually get from the meetings, but I couldn't contribute verbally. To this day, very little English is spoken in corporate Japan, yet they are all admired in the western culture and many times knew more about it than me.

During my first stint in Tokyo, I bumped into another colleague from the university, Tsiel, at 3 am at some club in Tokyo. He had grown up in America, France and Israel and ended up working for Toshiba as a software engineer. Later, when I came back with my new wife, we kept in touch and he told me he had found a job with UBS Banking. The thought of working in an English-speaking environment and career prospects lead me to join the financial industry in Tokyo. After several interviews, I landed a job in Jardine Fleming, Asia's financial powerhouse, the centre of the book *Noble House*. I was, with one step, suddenly deep into the real corporate world. It was a tough adjustment for an ex-farmer tank commander from Israel, but the package was great and we finally could start saving some real money for our future.

I worked with Anthony and Neil. Anthony headed the quant team and ran a quant trading book. Neil was a bright and cocky 25-year-old with a PhD from Cambridge and a typical English eccentric. We later became very good friends. I developed real-time trading systems and hung around with the trading team. One day, Anthony called me to the board room. His wife was having their second child and she had just left back to London.

He had a couple of weeks before he would follow and he asked me if I wanted to take over with his guidance from London. I knew all the technical terminology and the math, but I had zero background in financial markets. I said, "I'm in," like most crazy things in my life, not really knowing how I was going to handle it. Before I knew it, I was to take over a GBP100m trading book that was having a serious health problem. We decided to clear most of the book and start again. I will never forget my first trade ever. It was a few future contracts and I wrote the ticket and submitted the order. The boss from London was next to me. He leaned over and asked, "Ram, are we selling or buying?" As he finished, I realised I had executed the opposite trade. I was nearly in tears, but I reversed it as soon as I could and managed to make a few thousand dollars in the process. I knew it was definitely a beginner's luck!

Within a few weeks, I had built some confidence and started trading big. Coming from a computers and math background, I always treated trading as numbers rather than money. It worked to my advantage in trading and against me in my personal life, where the money had a short life expectancy. I moved into real-time quant trading unaware that while I was realising real-time large trades into the market quietly, the entire Flemings' trading floor was jumping a few seconds later, screaming WTF. Who is trading there? The guys realised they needed to get closer to me and try and understand what kind of quant trades I was doing. To date, I think the majority of them never had a clue why I bought or sold what I did, but it worked well for me.

One day, we had to test new real-time algorithms with the stock exchange. Testing was done on weekends when the markets were closed, however, most trading houses participated to test their systems. It was invisible to the outside world, but for us, it appeared just like the market was open and trading. I set up with our Japanese tech team and started testing. Testing is quite boring with various testing scenarios and outline cases. Finally, I asked the guys what the capacity of the system was in terms of large trades. I was told that technically the system could handle around a trillion Yen, which was around 10 billion USD. As per usual, it had to be tested by me. Before anyone could stop me, I unleashed a 10-billion-dollar trade into the stock market. Within seconds, phones started ringing and the stock exchange was halted. My Japanese tech team was running out of oxygen, yet it had worked. It was just testing and no harm was done, but no one had ever dared to test the limits of the stock exchange servers. Naturally, it was the first thing that came to my mind. I turned around to the team and told them, "It is working."

I will talk a little in the book about financial markets and trading as it was a significant part of my life in various roles. From a programmer to a CEO of a public company, I still miss the action and the stimulating environment, but I never liked the culture and what money did to people. It certainly affected me as well later on, but I tried hard to keep a clear head and not let money and greed drive my actions or my trades. Very few people outside the banking industry understand what is going on in the market. The visible part is like a small window of a massive maze of action, trades, deals and interest. The power that industry has still fascinates me though. The industry as a whole provides a vital service to the world economy, yet most people working in the industry are not focused on any big picture. They are focused on maximising gains.

I matured very quickly realising how naïve I was and that most people are about the economy. As a proprietary trader (trading for the bank, not for clients) you need to understand the system very well and exploit price discrepancies. Once you quantify all the factors and there were many, you decide how much risk you can take and pull the trigger.

One of my smaller trades was a Japanese company whose stock was extremely illiquid. Someone was selling the stock daily but had no buyers. I picked it up and simply placed an order at 10% lower every afternoon. As the market closed the stock dropped to the only available buyer and I got my shares. I did this quietly for about seven days, building up a small share portfolio at cheaper and cheaper prices. I knew that at some stage it would correct itself. That is the beauty of the market. Everything that survives goes back to its real value.

One afternoon, after seven days, I saw the CEO and the head of equity sales approaching my desk. I was asked if I was involved in this company. I was trading, I don't think I even knew the name of the company or what it did, I simply exploited technical events in the system. Nothing illegal, yet the CEO of that company happened to be a good client of Flemings and after his company's share price collapsed around 40%+ in seven days, he called Flemings and asked the CEO for help. I stopped the trade and no one understood what I was doing. Yet, for me, it was a huge lesson that helped me later in my working life. Behind every stock you buy sell or trade, there is actually a company with employees, a team that's actually doing something real, such as building, manufacturing or innovating. There I was like some wizard with a magic wand, swinging their future up and down regardless of their success. I learnt an important lesson – make it your business to know and care. But the financial markets are ruthless and I have seen many times good businesses disappearing for showing some weakness during a tough period.

Lots of things happened in Japan. One of the most important of them was the birth of my first baby girl, Kaitlin. That was another event that changed my life forever and only for the better. She was the first of my four kids, all simply amazing and gave a beautiful meaning to my hectic life.

At office

However, after a few years, I started to feel the concrete fever. It was the only time in my life when I didn't live by the water. Sometimes we would get in the car and drive to the harbour or the sea just to have coffee by the water. Eventually, I requested to be relocated to Hong Kong. I started trading all over Asia to cement my case to move to Hong Kong, the Wall Street of Asia. And in 1994, we moved to Hong Kong. We found a small house on the beach in Discovery Bay, half an hour ferry ride to central. Jardine was the powerhouse of Asia at the time and we had the most magnificent 36-story building on the Victoria Harbourfront. It had one thousand huge round windows and the Chinese referred to it as the house with a thousand arseholes.

We changed our description from *gaijin* to *gwailo*, which meant ghost people or pale people (it has a few other meanings too…) Hong Kong was a refreshing change. It was semi-British although it was still a British colony. Many times, you could be in London and if you chose to, you could explore China. Chinese are very different from the Japanese mostly because they show emotions. Although I couldn't understand them any better, I could read them much better. Hong Kong was as crowded as an ant's nest, moving around almost on top of each other in millions, yet somehow, it all worked, traffic moved and everyone got to where they needed to.

I was now a senior trader, still learning a lot and I traded just about any country that was demonstrating trading opportunities. I didn't care if it was Lebanon, India or Bangladesh. Mostly through my own developed technical algorithms and own research, I traded. Flemings was never a trading house like Salomon Brothers (ex) or Goldman Sachs. I realised I was in the wrong culture, but by the time it happened, I had decided to go back to South Africa. I did my homework and traded, sometimes sending the back-office's admin team into a near coma by having to chase my trades and settle them around Asia. I always liked the big picture and never bothered with small trades. It was never an incremental small step that changes a person. It did backfire on me a few times over the years when it was required, but I did prefer to stick to what I knew best.

I was trading a big portfolio in the Thailand stock market one time. I developed a real-time system so I could watch my portfolio move every minute. I had market exposure in 14 countries and many different time zones. No lies it was very stressful. We didn't have cell phones, real-time systems or internet like today. The markets started trading from 6 am in Tokyo to 12 am in other markets. I was stretched and quite alone. The other guys didn't really understand my trades. I should have asked for assistance, but I was too independent and as per usual and tried to do it all by myself.

At some stage, I got hold of Long-Term Capital Management, a bunch of ex-super traders and professors, including a few names like Professor Myron Scholes (Nobel prize winner with Professor Black for their option pricing model) Robert Merton, the derivative of John Meriwether (the start of 'Liars Pokers') and a few other financial gods. They wanted to join in on the Thailand trades, however, they wanted to get involved in volumes of hundreds of millions of dollars, way too big for Thailand, and we had to sadly decline their trades.

One more thing started in Hong Kong. Something that would change my life forever…swimming. Suffering from two torn knee cartilages from a short stint in Aikido in Tokyo, I struggled to get back into martial arts. Hong Kong had a colourful martial art school, but they all did forms of Kung Fu and involved significant acrobatics that my knees couldn't handle. So, I joined the resident club on the island and started swimming. I started with ten lengths at a time on the way back from work. I swam two lengths and rested for five minutes, literally on the verge of cardiac arrest. It was the first time in my life I swam in a swimming pool. I had no idea about marathon swimming or competitive swimming, but I could swim, slowly. Ten lengths in a 25 m pool are 250 m. Nowadays, that is a joke for a swim. Today, I need at least 1000 m just to warm up, which would be in the pool or 2–3 km to warm up in the sea.

After two weeks, as I was swimming, a young lady jumped in my lane, told me to stay on my side and swam 40 lengths non-stop. My jaw dropped. I was so impressed I couldn't sleep. The next day, it was my turn. I decided to swim 40 lengths, non-stop. I nearly drowned but managed it. I was so proud of myself; I couldn't stop smiling. I always liked to look around to gauge 'what is possible'. I have big dreams, but I am a realistic person. Once I can see and understand how something is possible, it's just about the execution. I use it all the time, scanning the environment for amazing feats. Once I see how it's done, I try it. Age does present minor limitations over time, but I just scan different spectrums to understand what is possible. I started swimming 2 km a day, morning, at lunchtime or evening. It became a drug for me, or more like my meditation, and a time for cleansing.

After a good few years, I realised it was time to go back to the real world – Cape Town, South Africa. I turned down London and stayed in Hong Kong. Kim was pregnant with Joran, our second daughter, it was time to go home.

Chapter 9
Cadiz – A Bonfire of Vanities

At a function during my corporate days, before I lost my suit and shoes

When I came back to South Africa, nothing prepared me for what was about to come my way. Good and bad, hard and fun trust and betrayal, profit and loss. Another chapter in my life is about to begin.

After nine years in Asia, I was finally back in Cape Town. I always knew I would go back to South Africa. We would visit every Christmas and it always took my breath away when we landed looking at the ocean, Robben Island and Table Mountain. I still look at these beauties with rare appreciation every time I arrive back after a trip away. There is no doubt it is one of the most beautiful places in the world offering a dramatic landscape, an amazing expanse of water and uniqueness like no other. I still, after so many years, fall in love over and over with my Cape Town.

It was certainly an adjustment. I was back in the real world again. In Asia, everything had been covered by the company and back in South Africa, it was early 1996 and at the age of 39 with one child and one on its way, a tourist visa and no job, I had to, again, reinvent myself and my life. A new beginning is always a delicate matter. I had been there before and I would be there a few times again, later. It's never easy. It always looks exciting in hindsight and one does appreciate it, but when you are in the thick of it, you never know what is coming next and it can be quite challenging.

I had a good experience in the international financial markets and I thought finding a job would be easy. However, I had very little knowledge about the South African market and I was on a tourist visa. I was married, so it was easier to obtain a work permit, but it took me six years to get my South African citizenship. Luckily, we saved some money and we managed to buy our first house in Hout Bay.

Masters World Championship Christchurch, NZ

I started swimming with Cape Town masters in the Con-Constantia pool, which was my official start of joining the ranks of swimmers. It was the first time in my life I had trained in a swimming squad and I had to learn quickly all the pool etiquette. A lane with eight swimmers requires a strict code of conduct or it could turn into mayhem and 'there would be blood'. Later on, I learnt that pool swimmer have a very short tolerance capacity compared to open water swimmers. I fitted in fairly quickly and established the leisure life of morning swim followed by breakfast followed by the search for employment and some socialising.

I will never forget my first real ocean open water swim, which took place from Simons Town to Glencairn. It used to be a very popular route around 3 km hugging the beach, but since it was colonised by great whites and since an English regular swimmer was taken by a great white on the same beach, it lost its popularity. Nevertheless, there I was playing with the great whites.

I started the swim and very quickly ended up all alone. The wave size picked up and at one stage I wasn't sure where I was going. I had little experience in the big cold sea, but I wasn't afraid. The water temperature was around 15°C, which is now considered a very pleasant temperature for much longer distance swims. I remember feeling very cold, so cold that I started to worry. I waved and waved and eventually, a rubber duck materialised from somewhere. I also learnt later on the fact that you can't see anything doesn't mean no one can see you. An open water swimmer with some swell and waves is around 10 cm above water level with almost zero visibility. But the rubber duck is much higher and can track movement in the water. I panicked anyway, which was a dangerous place to be. The duck arrived and accompanied me around the corner as I swam. Once I saw the beach and the water calmed down, I was able to finish the swim in better spirits.

On exiting the water, I remained extremely cold. I couldn't talk or hold anything and Hester, an open swimmer good friend who happened to be on the beach, offered me a lift to Simons Town to collect my car. We stopped at the coffee shop overlooking Glencairn for hot chocolate and I couldn't even hold my cup, which resulted in Hester spoon-feeding me until I managed to sip some from the mug.

The Cold sea

That had been a real lesson of respect for the sea and the cold, which I will always remember. The second lesson was my first Robben Island attempt. At that stage, I still wasn't used to cold water. The water temperature was 13°C, nice and warm and I had to abort halfway as I was seriously hypothermic. It took me a good couple of hours to recover and it scared the hell out of me. I nearly decided to abort cold water swimming for good and go back indoors. Thank goodness I didn't.

Robben Island is a relatively short swim for long-distance swimmers, some 7.4 km, yet the conditions vary and make the swim difficult. A few years later, I crossed Robben Island with Andrew Chin and co. with no swimming cap and at a temperature of 10°C and stopped for a tot of tequila halfway. It was epic. A definite mind over matter experience.

In the meantime, the work front wasn't looking rosy. I went to several interviews and didn't like what I saw, especially the salary. The hedge fund strategies I traded in Asia were not possible in South Africa. The exchange was still manual and the market was too small and limited due to exchange controls. Spending years in a big financial corporate, I looked to start my own business or join a small shop and learn the local markets first. I had no desire to join the big established players in South Africa. I needed freedom! But that didn't happen.

One night, I went to see a movie with my brother, Amos, and a friend from The University of Cape Town, University of Cape Town. He mentioned a small financial start-up company called Cadiz and he gave me their number. I called the next day and went over for a chat. I ended up meeting a team of six trader brokers, an accountant, a quant and a secretary, all younger than me. The company had been started by Ray Cadiz from Zimbabwe, who recruited his younger brother, Frank, in 1993. They set up small equity estivates broking shop and in 1994, they recruited Steve Mckenna and Brian Curtis, two more Zimbabweans to set up a fixed income brokering desk. In 1996, a few months before my arrival, another two Zimbabweans joined Kevin Morley on the fixed income desk and Heath Cuthbertson on the equity desk. They also hired a bean counter named Evan Jones and an eccentric Israeli-Argentinian mathematician named Ariel Sumeruk. It was a small private company that worked hard and played hard. Cadiz had a very white Zimbabwean culture, which was new to me and I knew I would have to adjust and adapt again.

It was a good fit, but we had no idea what to do together. We had a few beers and parted ways. I really liked what I saw, so I spent the next two weeks working out a proposal. The biggest lesson I learnt while working in Asia for nine years was 'add value and you will be valued!' I finally drafted three pages proposal to start a structured products desk, which later morphed into Cadiz Asset Management. I met with the directors again and received an offer to join them. The salary was a fraction of what I had earned overseas, but I was on a mission. I wasn't looking for a salary, I was looking for a place I could add serious value and benefit from it as it grew. It was a brave decision by them to hire me and a big leap of faith, but it paid the company and shareholders many times over.

I had found a new home and great friends. Sadly, time, egos and money has destroyed most of it over time, nevertheless, it ended up being the only place I worked in South Africa albeit for an intense 16 years.

The guys were very busy and I had my desk, telephone, computer and not a clue how to get things going. Innovation was always easy for me, so I started to learn about the South African market and came up with a few ideas. I built a few models and started calling around. After six months, I was a few hours from booking my first deal when it all fell apart. I knew everyone was talking about whether I would ever add value, yet I did have the full support of the directors. Although I was older than everyone, I was treated in some ways as a young newcomer. There was respect though, but I was certainly far below the senior level of the food chain. It didn't bother me. I always prefer to be respected for what I create rather than for a title or a rank.

There were times when my patience was called on in a big way. For example, every time that we went for sushi, which was a few times a week, everyone, especially Ray, would lecture me about sushi and Japanese food. I had only lived in Tokyo for seven years, but for some reason, they couldn't grasp it. I had a very low tolerance for arrogance and bullshit, but I did have a high tolerance when it came to different cultures. I didn't get offended, mostly, by the very insensitive comments or remarks, but it did take me a while to smile. I also had no problem putting people in their place when I felt they had crossed the line. I suppose it was difficult for them to relate to my background, my Israeli army experience, my years of travel, my accent and my work overseas in places like Japan and Hong Kong. I was deep in a very homogenous white Zimbabwean culture, something I had to accept or die. Given all that, I was accepted and respected for who I was.

I created a few interesting and dynamic financial products with all the required math. The guys helped and supported me, but it was time to test it. We went to see the National Building Society Bank (NBS) in Durban. We met with the big brass and had a good meeting. I gave them all my spreadsheets and charts and they asked if I could create and price a financial product they had given to J.P. Morgan South Africa, a product J.P.M hadn't been able or didn't want to price. I said sure and the next day, I sent them the structure, charts and prices. We never heard from them again.

That had been a huge lesson in big corporate arrogance and a lack of respect towards a small start-up. Their arrogance made us hundreds of millions of rands in the years that followed and it was only because we decided to do it ourselves.

We went to see the government pension fund, the PIC. In those days it was still run by the old-fashioned Afrikaans guys, but very honest and competent. It was hugely powerful and the biggest investor in the South African market. While that hasn't changed much nowadays, it seemed to run on air then. The office was very modest and simple and the salaries were the same. I went with Steve and Kevin and I sat in the back of the car as the newcomer I was.

I clicked with the CEO immediately, Badie Badenhorst. He was well-read and informed about world affairs. We had a great chat about Hong Kong, the Asian economy and other stuff. I finally presented my product and he liked it. He asked for the costs we are charging and as I had done my homework, I told him 0.45%. One thing I must explain was that he was our fixed income desk, main and biggest client. As Badie heard my fees, he stood up, slammed down his notebook and said, "Well, we have nothing more to talk about then." But he did ask me if I could implement it in a certain structure. I replied, "Sure!" although I had no idea how to go about it…yet.

We left and got into the car. Steve and Kevin were pale as ghosts. They thought I had just blown their biggest client. You must understand that the fixed income business is a high volume low margin business. The fee I had just asked for was around ten times what they charge. After a few seconds of silence, I received a serious cold shower from Steve and Kevin. Possibly I developed my tolerance for the cold after that onslaught. They weren't nasty about it, but they were very worried. I wasn't. If we were to get that product and get paid what I had asked, it would have been the equivalent of what they had brought in over the last three years, all in one deal.

Over the next two weeks that followed, I worked on the structure with great help from the guys. A further two weeks later, we got on a plane again to Pretoria, which over time became an almost weekly destination for me for many years. I had the solution, the structure, the charts and everything. This time, Ray, who realised the huge potential of this deal, joined me. We decided beforehand that we were not going to mention the fees and when it was brought up, we would simply leave it up to the client to decide.

We had a long chat and a great presentation with Badie, who was a black strong coffee and thin cigar serial consumer. The room was filled with smoke and when he finally raised the issue of fees again, we told him it was a new structure and it was up to him. After the previous reaction to my fees of 0.45%, we were lucky to be back and to not have lost the client.

He lit another one of his thin brown cigars, sipped his coffee and said, "I think 0.50% would be a fair price." We nearly choked. It was bigger than what I asked for weeks before. It was a life-changing event for the company and it did change our lives dramatically.

Later on, he told us that he knew the going market price was around 0.50% for those types of new structures and he had just tested us. He liked us and we got the deal, simple. We kept straight faces and thanked him, booking out the next few days to finalise the deal. The value of this deal was larger than the total sum Cadiz had made since its inception. There was one sure thing though – we knew we were all going to get heavily intoxicated that night.

The next few days, looking back, were so intense we nearly died from stress. We had been suddenly thrown not only into the deep end but also into an abyss of challenge. We formed asset management within four days and we searched the internet for dozens of legal documents that were required to book such a deal. We were asked to sign an ISDA (International Swaps and Derivatives Association) agreement. No one knew what it was. I knew it was a heavy and long legal document from my Hong Kong days, but that was dealt with by the legal team. We all printed tons of pages of legal documents and we had to read and understand them all. We were a small broking firm and suddenly overnight, we were asset managers, investors and fund managers with a legal team and we had to make it happen.

I'll never forget when Ray and I walked into Investec Bank, in March 1997, with a client cheque for half a billion rand and asked to open an account. South African financial markets were still much behind the international market's sophistication as it was only three years of democracy and there was a slow lifting of all sanctions. That first investment from the government pension fund of 500 million rands changed our lives forever and I can proudly state that it grew to over 20 billion Rands by 2012.

That deal created a chain of business within the company that later on lead to great growth, success, greed and entitlement. I always believed that money and success changed people. Some can carry it humbly, some blow it, and some just enjoy it and what it offers, but everyone changes. It certainly affected me as well, a farm boy from a small kibbutz, but I was very much aware of it and although I did find myself puffing my chest sometimes, I do owe it to my swimming which again taught me humility and what is real in life. I still, today, cannot fathom how people judge others by their wealth rather than by their substance. It is something we never get taught in school or in life. Money and wealth are great. It can bring huge freedom and opportunities, but since we are finite limited human beings, the amount of wealth required to make us happy and free is actually not as nearly as much as everyone desires. Don't get me wrong, I am not an aspiring Shaolin monk, but I have very little attachment to assets, cars, houses etc…I have a great attachment to experiences, quality of life and my family.

I grew up in a near pure socialist environment and I didn't like it. Even there, underneath the 'socialism' invisibility cloth I saw a lot of greed and I chased substance rather. I call it the 'Kardashian syndrome', yet they haven't invented it, they simply exploit a very old human disease. I probably have offended many people over the years and probably will do so still by not paying the required respect to one's wealth and status acquired by one's wealth. I simply can't help it. As much as I try and as much as I can be impressed sometimes by wealth and status, it is always short-lived and the minute I realise there is no substance beneath the form, I lose respect. Wealth and IQ or talent are not correlated. I have met too many wealthy people who, for whatever reason, were convinced that the wealthier they were, the higher their IQ and talent were. That attitude is the main reason for many successful small start-ups collapsing the day when ego meets reality. Cadiz was heading in that direction already, blissful and drunk with success.

I was made a director and received some shares in the company significantly less than I was promised and asked for though. Looking back, it was that moment that I should have left and started my own shop as most people in the market had done. But I felt an immense loyalty to the guys who had hired me and had given me the opportunity. I also had to consider then that I had a family, two children at that time. I was grateful but also naive.

There was no doubt that we had great fun and we were a great bunch of people, however, the culture that was created was way too arrogant and fluffy. We got stuck for years in our teenage stage and we never managed to come out of it in a mature way. It created a culture of entitlement and greed. We simply made too much money and it was too easy, in some ways. That drove us to list on the stock exchange and grow exponentially with less and less value add. This form of behaviour and growth is very common for start-up companies. Many small successful start-ups fail to rise from that. Many sell at the top and avoid failure. People made vast amounts of wealth yet created very little substance. Some of these people end up running big countries.

Nevertheless, we chased more business and we landed a second deal with the government pension fund. It was a similarly huge deal, but it was on condition that the deal was done with an international bank to diversify credit exposure. We agreed on the terms with a big international bank and we headed back to Cape Town.

It was the company Christmas party. Everyone knew about it and was waiting for us in Uitsig, private dining room. The company, at that stage, was still small, end of 1997, the party consisted of ten staff and their partners. I rushed to the party, picking up my wife, Kim, on the way. En route from the airport, I had to field five calls from the bank stating that they couldn't do the deal. When I arrived at the party, Ray pitched up too. Everyone was welcoming us like heroes. That second deal meant a huge amount to our future. I couldn't bring myself to tell anyone that the deal was possibly falling apart. It was time to celebrate, regardless.

Hours later, with the significant help of the house vino, I climbed on the main table and decided to try and mimic the table dance from the movie *Hair*. I was drunk and needed to release the stress. Luckily, everyone rushed ahead and managed to clear the table as I traversed it and only a few plates ended up flying around. Once the table was clear, the whole company, around 15 of us, ended up dancing on the table at the most prestigious venue in Cape Town. It was great fun and needless to say, we didn't manage to impress the manager. As things quietened down a bit, I dragged Ray, the CEO, to the side and updated him. I'm not sure if he got it or even if he wanted to hear it, but I did tell him, "We are going to London tomorrow morning as we need to find another bank."

The next morning at 8 am with a severe hangover, I called our Personal Assistant, Margaret, and asked her to book us on the next flight to London. It was Saturday and we would be arriving in the big city on Sunday. We had a meeting on Wednesday morning in Pretoria to sign the deal and I spent the entire day arranging meetings for Sunday and Monday with every big bank I knew in London. I briefed them on the deal and set times to meet.

Ice bath

The only ticket Margaret could get at such short notice was British Airways first class. I didn't care. We had no choice. There was too much at stake. Margaret had to go to Ray's flat to wake him up and he had no recollection of the discussion from last night. He called me and I told him again that we had to go or we would have no deal. That sobered him up.

We packed and rushed to London, first-class, very nice. However, it completely escaped us that it was mid-December, summer in Cape Town but freezing cold in London. Again, serendipity, my cold training continued even though involuntarily.

The next few days were a roller coaster of events. One particular event saw us rushing to a meeting in the City of London, freezing cold with our summer suits and nothing else. About 100 m from the back main door, a window cleaner, 20 or 30 floors high, emptied his dirty water bucket on me. Aside from the fact that I nearly had a cardiac arrest from the shock, my suit was wet, filthy and I looked like a plucked duck. This was my first ever ice bath. It was very funny but the timing and the fact that it happened to me was not funny at all. I rushed inside, dried my suit and myself with the hand dryer in the toilet and proclaimed that we were ready. I certainly was hoping we were ready!

Long story short, we managed to catch the flight home to arrive just in time for the meeting in Pretoria. Badie had no idea what had transpired. When we told him, he said he had never seen someone so dedicated (or desperate). We ended up spending the entire day in his office. The London bank's legal team had insisted that the Minister of Finance had approved the deal. The Minister of Finance, at the time, was Trevor Manual and Badie couldn't get hold of him. Needless to say, he said he would just sign it over the phone. We tried everything. By that stage, Badie had finished two packets of his new thin cigars I had bought for him whilst in London. Coffee and smoke were pouring out of our ears and we were super wired but also tired like overcharged Duracell bunnies. Finally, we managed to find a solution and the deal was signed.

Our investment top performed out of 37 other similar structures the client had, which helped us plenty in the future. We had a few interesting episodes with those deals. The first one was on the first anniversary when we received an unexpected and definitely unaccounted for 1 million rands worth of interest on parts of the product. We called the client and delivered the good news. He just couldn't believe it. It was in our bank account, due to our dealings, but no one would ever know that. It wasn't ours. It was his and it was as simple as that.

Several years later when we had to restructure the deal due to changes in government funding, we had to liquidate the deal and reinvest it in a new structure of around 5 billion rand. That exercise generated an unexpected profit of 278 million rands. It was the accounting method that didn't use market value to price an investment, but its expiry value. The restructuring has crossed book value with market value and created an unaccounted-for profit. We assumed it was great news, however, it created a huge accounting problem for the client. I had several meetings for a few years trying to explain to the client's accounting army, where this profit had materialised from. For us, it was very simple. For the accountants, it was not possible.

I recall a meeting when I was told that if we kept it and never told the client they would never know and their lives would have been much simpler. It was right out of *Monty Python's The Meaning of Life*, that first episode about the British accounting firm. It never crossed our minds. It wasn't ours and again it was that simple. But I could see how the client feared this unexpected gift. It could have been the other way as well since accounting policies have changed to avoid these gaps that could lead to big surprises. It was a massive amount of money, yet never once did it cross our minds to try and keep it. It wasn't ours to keep, simple.

Freedom Swim, from Robben Island to mainland
I started it and ran it for 20y until Covid came

We listed the company in April 1999 and many things happened. Brian, one of the founding directors and a good friend died in a motorcycle accident just before the listing. At that stage, I was very involved in master swimming and Brian had been a strong swimmer, so I decided to start the BC mile swim in his memory. It has been 20 years now and it's still going.

Looking back, the listing was the beginning of our end. The listing made the few founders and myself very wealthy literally overnight, on paper. We were high profile and had delusions of grandeur. Success also breeds greed and jealousy. All that people could talk about was how much money someone made and how much money someone was worth. Many employees had a spreadsheet to calculate their worth every day. It was nothing new or bad, but it was the reality of the financial markets industry. You dealt with money all day. You dealt with calculating money and margins all day. Your day was measured strictly by how much money you made on the day. It wasn't everyone. The culture created was not for everyone. The hype and the buzz had its benefits, but it also created a machine that was powered by hot air and distorted reality. It was intoxicating and poisoning at the same time. In those days, culture was well soaked with alcohol. Drinking copious amounts almost daily and playing just as hard was part of your evaluation process. We had boundaries. Nothing like the wolf of wall street, but the pace was hard.

My area at work has become the cash cow of the entire business. We hired people left and right and many didn't stay. Many came to us for the get-rich-quick ride rather than the challenge and innovation. Yet, we attracted some very talented and bright people. We had some great times when things went our way and we were rewarded for our innovation and products.

With success, politics grew. We hired experienced people from large organisations who had never created anything in their life. They managed and they tried to manage me. Big mistake! I am not a manageable type. I need direction, space and some resources and then I create. I was never a good manager and it is the first thing a 'good manager' does to point it out to you. It is that focus that starts eroding innovation in a business. It is difficult to argue with experience, mountains of management, leadership books and very competent consultants. Yet, the most important ingredient to success, as learnt through the years and still learning, is self-belief. It is one's ability to see through the fog, the mountains and the obstacles and notice that there is a beach on the other side with roads and trees and success. I still firmly believe that this mindset is the most important ingredient in achieving anything huge or impossible. All the rest are very important tools to manifest the challenge into success, but if you don't believe it and if you can't see it, it is all up to luck and hope, almost like a gamble.

I started finding solace in my swimming. I went to a few master's national championships and a few world championships. I left my name behind in each national championship as the misbehaving one. Nothing bad, just a little too adventurous. I never placed anyone at risk, my first rule, but I have placed myself at some risk a few times.

At the East London Nationals, after swimming and after happy hour, I decided it was time for some high diving. I, somehow, managed to climb over the barbed wire closest to the high dive tower, fully clothed, mind you. I just walked off the 10 m board into the air. I do remember many looking up with their mouths wide open. I landed on my backside and managed to surface next to my shoes (it was before the no-shoe days). I was in pain but nothing I couldn't manage. I was, of course, under the influence of some local alcohol and couldn't understand why everyone was so stressed. The next day, I swam the 400 m free, my whole backside down to the back of my knees was one huge blue bruise. I did a good time and enjoyed the swim, but I did struggle to sit down for a couple of days after.

Another naughty incident that comes to mind was in the Pretoria National Championship. After happy hour, we all stripped naked and raced across the pool width up and down above the lane ropes. When we reached the end of the pool, I took a deeper dive than was required and I still remember the sound of my skull smashing into the pool floor. I surfaced, a little dazed and to everyone's horror with my face covered in blood, which was streaming from the gash in my skull. It wasn't as bad as it looked and I had no problem racing the next day. I did, however, leave my underwear floating somewhere and someone hung them half-mast at the start. The announcer kept on inviting the owner to come and collect them, but I chose to release this pair from my inventory and keep my anonymity. In Durban, I fell backwards at the Hilton Hotel entrance into a big cactus decorating the entrance. I still have that vivid memory of ripping my pants off then and there, with Jody and a good swimmer friend, plucking the painful thorns from my throbbing rear end.

A few years later, in Riccione, Italy, at the world championship, I got an asthma attack at the end of the 200 m individual medley. No one noticed or knew and I somehow climbed out of the pool, crawled outside and managed to calm down. I passed out for two hours in the shade by a big tree.

That was the end of my master's swimming. I was already venturing into open water swimming and adventures. Because of my swimming expeditions, Cadiz had already become synonymous with open water swimming in South Africa. Hardly anyone at the firm actually realised that or saw the benefit in it. It got to a place where Telkom ^0dropped South African swimming sponsorship and ownership and approached me at Cadiz.

A few years on and I started the freedom swim, the annual Robben Island crossing to Blouberg beach and the freedom swim series. I believe it played a huge role in growing open water and cold water swimming in South Africa. It has never made me a cent and probably cost me a lot, including the time invested, but it was a passion, something I realised was missing at Cadiz. There was a lot of noise and rumble, but it wasn't driven by passion. Without passion, there could be no success. In 2004, Andrew Chin approached me and asked me if I was keen to swim the entire length of the Orange River, 2000 km. The timing was right and anyway, it was not my style to turn down a good adventure and a challenge. I replied, "I'm in."

That probably started my swimming adventures that later took over my life and still does. I never looked back once!

Back to Cadiz. Although we did very well for many years and we mostly made loads of money, but our innovation declined. Staff entitlement grew, led by management entitlement, egos soared together with costs and our soul was beginning to fade. A vast majority of our revenue came from the source of these initial deals and a few spin-offs.

I became the CEO in late 2005 and it was both great and bad. Company politics was already rife. My transition to the CEO position wasn't a simple one. Most times, taking over from the founder has very little chance of success unless he disappears or you follow his instructions. Neither happened. It was a tough ride trying to lead the company and trying to watch my back. The board was caught in the middle and at the end of the day, it didn't really know how to deal with this. In hindsight, I should have left much earlier or taken a much tougher stance. I always felt indebted for having been given this opportunity, so taking a ruthless hard stance just didn't work for me. I simply couldn't do it.

The Atlantic Ocean survival swim – me on the right

I always lead Cadiz with what I believed was the best interest of the company at heart, not mine. Some would say it was a naïve way of running a business because you could lose your place while fighting for the company.

However, I have no problems looking at myself in the mirror every morning. I always felt that my conscious was clean. Did I make mistakes? Plenty! But I did care for the people of the company dearly and tried my best to make their lives exciting, stimulating a rewarding.

As we succeeded, we grew and our culture struggled to adapt to our changing reality. We grew from 15 staff to over 200 in a short space of time with no compelling commercial need. There was a culture that if you just hired good people, they would find a way to create and make money. I believed in new products, quality and innovation but many focused on profit, sales and making love to their egos, as David Bowie sang.

2008 saw me heading off to Antarctica and I completed my first real ice swim. Later on, I received a Guinness World Record acknowledgement for that, which pissed off Lewis immensely. Tough luck, I say. I have always believed that records are put there to be broken and challenge others to excel.

In 2009, I started the International Ice Swimming Association. I funded it from my own pocket and tried hard to not let it interfere with my work and at the same time, I hoped to inspire my staff. Some admired it and some saw it as Ram fulfilling his dreams rather than focusing on his work.

Youngsters at work started to ask me what I actually did. Some never made a cent for the firm and didn't realise their daily profits and clients had come from deals originated and driven by me. I tried to let those deals go. I tried to delegate and move into new areas. It was a big mistake and a lesson that was hard to take in but taught me a lot.

When I looked around at the amazing successes, it was mostly driven by very few individuals that had a 'hand-on' style. The others simply added no value. I still believe in that management style. Hands-on! Roll up your sleeves and get involved! If you think that you can simply pass your success on to others and sail into the sunset, don't be surprised to find anything when you get back. There are many talented and competent people everywhere. But when you succeed in something, you either sell it at the top or drive it. By simply hiring talents to drive it for you has very little chance of success. It doesn't mean that they are incompetent or less talented, but it wasn't their creation, therefore, many times, they will not create or succeed in places you would have. It doesn't mean you do it alone, never, but maybe because I grew up in real socialism and saw it collapse and corrupt, saw it as a creator of mediocrity I never believed in it.

Yet, as good as the money was with no passion, it was very difficult to lead. I realised my days in Cadiz were numbered. I had my life invested in the firm and my life wealth, even though it was mostly paper wealth. I couldn't leave without making sure that my future was secured. And so, in 2006, I drove the acquisition of African Harvest's fund management. We had cash and asset management. We suddenly jumped up to be a real player in the asset management business. If done right, that business, as some say, could be a licence to print cash. An average asset management business receives annual fees and if it does well, it can also rip a windfall of performance fees. As long as you survive and have the critical mass of assets and a reasonable team, you could be fine. It is never as simple as that, but it is significantly easier than making iPhones or cars.

At the time, Cadiz had 65 billion rands of assets while Coronation had around 80 billion. Ironically, about eight years later, Coronation had over 500 billion rands worth of assets under management and Cadiz had only close to 20 billion, now days it has almost disappeared completely.

My last stint was to sell our securities business that was struggling to an international bank. It was a fascinating deal and a real challenge. It could have been a possible launch pad to our securities business or its end, but at least we got an extremely good deal. The board didn't really understand where Cadiz was heading towards to. Cadiz was sucked into a political turmoil driven by the main shareholders. These types of scenarios mostly lead to one outcome. There are no winners in that sort of scenario, everyone loses. I should have left long ago, but, alas…I didn't.

In the next few years, my departure from Cadiz followed by my second divorce dropped me into a serious abyss financially and in many other aspects. If it wasn't for my four wonderful kids and the ice swimming, I possibly would have drowned. But I didn't!

Chapter 10
How I Met the Cold Sea

It was Christmas, 1994 and we were visiting Cape Town, friends and family. We were still living in Tokyo, Japan, at the time but we always made sure we came back to Cape Town for Christmas. Tokyo was icy and grey and Cape Town was sunny and blue; there wasn't really a choice. How things have changed though? Nowadays, I hardly ever spend Christmas and New year in Cape Town. I simply can't take the heat and the crowds.

We ventured out with the family to Scarborough to a quiet and beautiful beach. Kaitlin, who was two years old then could play on the sand protected from the wind and waves. I decided to venture into the sea. A walk on the beach and barefoot in the shallows didn't take long to cause me a headache. Nevertheless, I dived in and went off to play in the surf. I was very cold, but the hot sun compensated for the icy feeling and I managed to play around for around 20 minutes. I clearly recall going through some freezing pain and settling in after around five to seven minutes in a very comfortable space. The water temperature was around 10°C.

Years later, I realised my skin had just gone numb, my head adjusted and for around ten minutes, I felt so wonderful and alive. Soon the icy water penetrated my bones and I felt frozen solid. I got out and recovered on the beach, shivering in the sun. Cape Town sun is one of the strongest I have ever encountered due to the thin ozone layer. In Israel, it would take hours to cause the same damage the Cape sun can do in 30 minutes. On the beach, I thought to myself that the water wasn't that cold. But when I tried again later, I lasted for a few seconds before ejecting my icy body from the surf in serious agony.

It took me many years to learn about the cold and to be able to respect it. I cannot say I will ever master and tame it, but I certainly have learnt to coexist with mutual respect, well, at least I hope the ice has some respect for me. But it probably is more amused and has a good chuckle whenever I try and survive it. The ice always wins! I have never doubted that or claimed to conquer it, but I have learnt to not be scared of it and to create some relationships and friendships forever.

My first true encounter with the cold was in 1996. I had enough of Asia and I needed to get back to nature. So, I resigned from Hong Kong to everyone's surprise and declined an offer to move to London or Zurich as I needed to rekindle my life-long relationship with the sea, fresh air and fewer people.

Living for nine years in Tokyo and Hong Kong certainly developed some claustrophobic tendencies in me. I had enough brushing with a few millions of people every day. I was born in nature and I realised I had paid my dues to the big concrete jungle. I had had enough.

And so there I was, swimming in Cape Town's master's squad. It was good fun and good training, but I was fascinated more by this other breed of swimmers who swam in the cold ocean. Clifton cold mile was one of the ultimate challenges. My brother, Amos, who was swimming regularly those days, told me how he swam it once with his wife, Revi, on the kayak next to him. The water temperature was just 11°C and he somehow managed to finish it, stone last and in serious hypothermia. He couldn't remember how he did it. Amos, being an ex-navy seal and a professional diver, wasn't easily intimidated by this. I certainly was. Nevertheless, I joined a group of swimmers swimming in Clifton once a week to get used to the cold water and train for the Robben Island crossing.

Back then, the Robben Island crossing was as remote as a one-way expedition to Mars. It was so remote I wasn't even fascinated by it. It belonged to a different breed of people, the very few that possessed physical and mental abilities belonged to demigods, as far as I was concerned then. Michael Angelo once said, 'Every rock has an angle inside. I just curve it out…' (or something like that. I just love that comment and I, later on, adopted it in my work and extreme swimming life. Another quote that stuck with me was, 'Everyone has a superhuman inside them. They just need to set it free…'

Back in Clifton, we used to swim for 20 minutes and get out solidly frozen. It was the first time I was exposed to frozen fishing stories – people who swam here and there and had done amazing things in the cold. Some, like all fishing stories, were true and correct and some were urban legends, where water temperatures dropped to 1°C every time the story was retold. Waves grew by a foot each time and eventually, some big sharks joined the legend. Luckily, I am built with a very healthy dose of cynicism in me and when the fish seem too big to be real, I go and investigate them.

Swimming my Robben Island Double

From the beginning, I was just listening and watching. You can learn a lot from just observing. People's ability in the water, their reaction to the cold, their stroke, their breathing, listening to their experiences and more importantly, their recovery. I was already realising that this was completely unchartered territory. There were so many different experiences and the actual facts told another story altogether. If the cold is so deadly, how come many people around the world do amazing swims, like the English Channel and other long cold swims? The cold definitely had my attention!

I started pushing my swimming in the sea and set my eyes on the Robben Island crossing. It was around 1998 when I attempted my first crossing and it was the annual Robben Island crossing event with around 20 odd swimmers. It was run by Vista Nova School for children with learning disability and was started by a mother of one of the kids and her husband, a fearless open water swimmer. Around a few years later, the event collapsed due to a lack of sponsorship. That was when I stepped in with Cadiz as the main sponsor and turned it into what it is now although after I left Cadiz, they didn't want to stay in. It then became my personal event and is known now as the world-famous 'freedom swim'.

I started the swim from Robben Island with water temperatures of 13°C and I was okay to start with. I expected the cold shock and waited for it to settle down but didn't know much about cold in those days. At temperatures of around 15°C and above, the cold takes a long time, maybe hours, to get inside you. It cools down your skin and you remain in a long period of discomfort, for hours, but you have to get on with it.

When the water temperature drops to 13°C and below, it has a certain bite and not the same bite that comes with 10°C and lower. And certainly not the bite that comes with 5°C and lower. Every drop in Celsius degrees has its own bite. I got used to recognising it and today I can use my body to measure the temperature with very good accuracy. When the water gets to 13°C and below, the bite gets some sting in it, tingles your skin and burns. It takes around five minutes to settle in and your skin goes numb. What a wonderful feeling! The pain goes and a wonderful sensation, almost a glow emanates from your skin. It is like touching fire. When you are down to 5°C and lower, that sensation increases and you feel like you are in and out of the flames of a fire. I call it the 'fire in the ice'.

Once your skin is numbed by the cold swimming, it gets easier and more comfortable although the word comfortable has a different meaning when swimming in the cold. As you continue to swim, the cold starts to penetrate your bones or at least that's exactly how it feels. Little by little the cold starts to shut you down and around one and a half hours into my first Robben Island attempt, I was officially frozen, mentally and physically. I aborted the swim with the help of the boatman and the second. I was dragged up into the boat covered with blankets and I started to shiver uncontrollably for the next hour. It was a reality check and a scary one at that. These reality checks can break you if you are not committed. However, the human brain has a wonderful survival mechanism that brushes failures, smudges them and blurs them and at the same time highlights the good moments, the positive parts of your experience. I believe we all have it, or else we would be still in the cave, looking out with fear and waiting for food to come to our cave doorsteps.

I continued to train and a few months later, I was on the golf course, hacking the ninth hole with immense frustration, wishing I was at the 19th hole already. It was the Milnerton golf course, which overlooks Robben Island. I suddenly had a call from Judy, a master swimmer friend, "Ram, we are swimming Robben Island tomorrow with Andrew. John Green is our pilot."

I muttered the few choice French swear words I knew and said, "Okay!" I turned and told the guys I would not join them for the 19th hole after all. The torture after a heavy piss-up the night before would not go down well for a swim the next day.

The next day, we met early at Oceana. It was Andrew Chin, Judy Brewis and me. The legendary late John Green was our skipper. We ventured to Robben Island in the fog and as we arrived, we greased ourselves down, dived in and started swimming. The water temperatures were a balmy 16°C, which nowadays is considered almost too hot to handle.

The swim was simply epic. I loved it! I enjoyed it so much that I managed two hours and 12 minutes of swim time. It taught me a huge lesson in the cold – never give up and carry on collecting positive experiences. Don't worry too much about the negative ones, they will find you, unwelcome and unsolicited and when they get you, take it, learn from it and move on to the next one. The cold was never about winning or conquering; it was always about sharing my experiences with the water, and the sea. I never fooled myself that I could beat the cold or tame the ice. Maybe it was my science education and understanding of thermodynamics and the conservation of energy.

For me, every time I have a great swim in the cold or the ice, I almost thank it for allowing me in and sharing it with me. The ice and the cold never give anything for free. Over time, I have learnt to deal with the tax that the cold imposes. I have taken the time to study it and to understand it better. But most importantly, I learnt not to fear it but rather to only understand and respect the cold.

The cold continued to fascinate me. At that stage, Andrew attracted my attention to Lynne Cox's book *'Swimming to Antarctica'*. I read the book and took note of the swims, which inspired us later on to follow and complete a few of the swims. But mostly it inspired me to start my passion for chasing the ice.

In Cape Town, in the meantime, Lewis started his career as an extreme swimmer and a cold and ice water chaser. Lewis had a different agenda though and he focused on the surroundings, the environment and the global warming aspect. He started his business model, which later on made him a world-renowned activist. Lewis invited me to his swims in the Norway Fjords and I invited him back to second a few of my colder swims.

I recall my first attempt to do the swim from Llandudno to Camps Bay, a 10 km swim, which was across the shoreline with the 12 apostles mountain range in sight. We met in Llandudno and I was supposed to swim with Andrew and Francoise, however, the boat broke down en route from the launch in Hout Bay. I did swim another route of around 10 km a few years later though. The water temperature was 9°C. In hindsight, we were far from ready to attempt a 10 km swim in that temperature. Nevertheless, we swam around for 45 minutes. When we came out, headstrong and feeling very much cold and alive, Lewis asked me "Why, Ram? What are you after? You already proved you have a very strong mind." Some answers in life, for roads driven by some unexplained passion, come to you later on and shed better clarity of what was driving you at the start. I replied, "I am just fascinated with the cold water."

Lewis warned me several times later on, "Your mind will be your weakness, it can kill you." I was very well aware that I had a strong focused mind. I spent five years in the active army and I was a hedge fund trader. I also knew a lot about risk, studying it, analysing it, quantifying it and riding it in a very calculated way. I knew I was just starting my cold journey, but I had no idea how far it would take me and many others around the world. Death never scared me, but boredom terrified me.

I continued to explore the cold water of Cape Town, and the trip to Antarctica in February 2008 was the point that changed my life and many other lives forever.

Antarctica is in another chapter and there are many more to come. I have been to Antarctica, swimming, three times now and I can't wait to go again. As bizarre as it may sound to some, for me Antarctica is the most beautiful place on earth. Probably because very humans are allowed there. We, humans, have a tendency to destroy beautiful raw nature. It's a real shame.

My swim in Antarctica certainly scared me as it was really intense and mind-blowing. But at the same time, it created a complete paradigm shift in my understanding of the cold. I realised it wasn't the domain of someone with supernatural powers or abilities, it was possible for us mere humans.

A year later, I somehow managed to convince Andrew to join me to swim in Lake Geneva. To seal the deal, a fellow Cape Town swimmer, living in

Zurich, persuaded me to swim there. The Lake Zurich swim is also another chapter, however, I approached it with a mathematical linear mindset. I swam 1 km at 0°C, then tried to do 2 km at 1–2°C and 3 km at 3–4°C. I knew I could swim 8 km at 10°C, so swimming the 3 km at 4°C seemed achievable. Later on, I realised that the cold penetration is driven by a different thermodynamic formula that is significantly more exponential than linear.

The day before the swim, we walked the swim route along the Lake Zurich promenade. It was grey and cold and around -7°C. When we walked the 3 km there and back, we realised the walk itself was rather long and cold and we were fully dressed and relatively warm. I looked rather for a good safe starting location and the swim was cut short to 2.3 km.

The swim, the next day, took me 43 minutes. Andrew, who had never touched ice water before decided that 1.2 km was plenty. He wasn't in great shape when he finished, but he had made his first ice swim, a huge achievement. I pushed and with four support boats, I managed to finish it too.

The recovery and the experience brought home the very real boundaries of swimming in water temperatures for prolonged times that are close to zero. I was close to the edge of the abyss. I have had a few close brushes with death before. But how close? You never know because it can take a split of a second to cross the line of no return. It can be a scary place but it is also a place where extreme sportspeople have to explore in order to be able to push further.

I always remind myself of a quote from the book Dune by Frank Herbert about fear. It made a huge impression on me as a young teenager: *"I must not fear. Fear is the mind-killer. Fear is the little death that brings total obliteration. I will face my fear. I will permit it to pass over me and through me. And when it has gone past, I will turn the inner eye to see its path. Where the fear has gone there will be nothing. Only I will remain."*

Staring fear in the eye

I still don't know how far I could carry on swimming before I pass out or sink. For that swim, I was still moving slowly forward towards the stairs where the swim would end. I recall every second of the recovery and not for one second did I not know where I was. I recall ordering everyone around to assist me with my recovery. I still do that today, mind you.

Later on, in my swimming adventures, I saw swimmers who lost their memory or even their vision for a period, which apparently is 'quite normal under the circumstances' as the doctors in my medical forum said to me.

As insane as it may sound, I believe it is the path that paves the way for many extreme sports. Watching the incomprehensible massive waves the guys surf nowadays in Nazari, Portugal and other locations around the world, I know there are no shortcuts or miracles or genetics that suddenly allow one to do these seemingly utter mad things. They all look at the 'impossible' or the 'off-limits – deadly' areas in their sport and they study them. Quietly and slowly, I try and understand how they work.

Most, or just about all of us, would dismiss the massive waves and will rather focus on the 'fun'. For a few, 'fun' is not enough. They are not suicidal or just thrill-seekers, but they are fascinated. They don't like the concept of 'off-limits'. They want to understand why rather than just obey the norm. They understand the fear very well, but they are not scared. And then they venture, they make mistakes, they learn more, they try again and the real heroes are the ones who know they will never master it, control it or tame it. They are just simply privileged to be able to ride it for a little longer, for a little bigger, a little faster and a little colder. It is quite important to try and avoid death in the process, it limits the learning process.

That swim, which was carefully monitored by another mad extreme athlete, Professor Beat Knechtle, was the spark that started the International Ice Swimming Association. When I came back, after a few more adventurous days of skiing in Davos nearby, the concept was already brewing in my mind. I knew I was just starting, just scratching the surface. I knew I wanted to understand more and do more, but I realised that it required serious study and understanding and most important of all, safety parameters and limits. I wanted to share it to see how far we could go, and how much more we could learn about it.

Chapter 11
Recovering from an Ice Swim

End of Svalbard Glacier Ice Mile, 79 near the North Pole

Many have tried to describe the recovery process after an ice swim. Some will say it was 'an out-of-body experience', others 'a bad trip' or 'a black rain'. But mostly, it is a very personal experience because it is a hard and painful process.

We all deal with it differently from the physical aspect right to the mental. For me, the possibility of a hard recovery is always part of my swim and my planning. My swim ends when my recovery ends. When I push further into the ice, I take into consideration that I have to come back and it will be steeper.

It is a fascinating element of this mad and frozen sport that requires better understanding and experience. In fact, a great swim with a really bad recovery is not a great swim. No recovery is pleasant, but severe recovery tells its own story about your condition before you even started the swim. I always have a rule of thumb, which I apply to all my swims – 'I want to come out dignified.' It means to me that regardless of being solidly frozen sometimes, I am still here. I am aware that when attempting an extreme challenge, in any extreme sport, one pushes to the utmost limits. For me, in the ice, the utmost limit is the sum of the swim and the recovery. I see recovery as an integral part of the swim.

The theory behind the recovery or post-ice swim process is not new to most. If you have done a few ice swims of 20 minutes or longer in water temperature of 5°C or less, you have experienced it up close and personal.

The professional medical fraternity dealing with us at these swims are, mostly, not swimmers. They deal with our recovery, in the same manner, they would deal with any mild or severe hypothermia patient, which is the correct and professional protocol. Their focus is on rewarming the patient and monitoring all vital signs until all stabilises and gets back to the 'normal' range. The process of recovering from a hypothermic person is not a new one. There are a lot of experienced people in the field out there.

We are all aware of the importance of our core body temperature, however, the most accurate way to measure it is with a rectal thermometer. Ever tried chasing a recovering swimmer with a rectal thermometer? Good luck with that. Some doctors, whom I tend to agree with, claim that core body temperature after a mile swim is not the most important but that the brain core temperature is most critical. And in the same vein, try chasing down an ice miler, post a swim, with an invasive brain probe. Good luck again. Sval.

I always saw ice swimming as a huge mental challenge rather than just a physical one. It was always that facet that fascinated me the most and still does. I have done many recoveries personally and saw many more. In all the events I participate in, I try and check on every single swimmer as they go through recovery. I let the doctors do their thing and I am not there to replace them but more to assist the swimmers mentally and to learn. In a way, I see the medical staff's role as one to examine the swimmers for emergencies, possible problems and monitor recovery. I don't think it is required for the medical staff to be on-site to perform the recovery unless the swimmer requires medical assistance or attention. Until such time, anyone with experience in ice swimming and recovery can assist the swimmer in process of recovery. I have managed my own recoveries in all my swims with doctors and medical staff close on site.

I look at the eyes! They tell me everything I need to know. Many focus on core body temperature and vital signs such as pulse and blood pressure and, if needed, insist on an ECG, all critically important to assess if the swimmer requires medical attention or is at risk. I would like to clarify that I don't like the excess use of medical terms (for us, not medical professionals) and I would never claim to replace the medical process.

I generally assume that the swimmer is not in danger and is being overseen by the medical staff on site. I then focus on making my own recovery a less painful and more understood process. I also would like to distinguish between what we refer to as recovery and medical recovery, which focuses on your core body temperature coming back to normal and that your vital signs are normal and stable. I focus on that horrible after-drop process that takes us on this roller coaster ride of recovery.

To illustrate this point, I would like to take you through a specific recovery experience I had during one of my swims in Norway in 0°C of frozen dam water with floating ice sheets I had to push away as I was swimming. I stayed in the water for around 30 minutes and had to swallow the temperature capsule before the swim. My core reading was 36, 5°C an hour before the swim. It climbed up to 37, 8°C just before the swim and then went down to 35, 4°C after the swim.

Shower after the swim

As usual, the after-drop came around five to six minutes later. I was sitting in a heated car being driven to a warm shower at a nearby farm. A few minutes later, while in the shower, my core started plummeting 1°C per minute, 34°C, 33°C, 32°C, 31°C and then it hit 30°C. That drop is called the rollercoaster that hits you post-swim. Thirty minutes later, my core went up by 1.3°C and then down again by 2.4°C, but the actual net drop was from 36.5°C to 35.4°C, which is only 1.1°C in 30 minutes!

Post swimming my core temperature dropped by 5.4°C in around nine minutes. That was a hell of a ride. But what fascinated me the most was the fact that ten minutes later, I came out of the shower in full control, smiling and joking, had dressed and was desperate for a wee dram. My core body temperature was 33.4°C. I was still cold inside but 100% clear and fine mentally, at least I thought so. I was aware that I was still in the zone, which is considered dangerous and the doctor followed me for another 30 minutes making sure I was fine. Now, don't get me wrong, 33. 4°C is not normal and not safe. But I was 'fine', focused, 100% in control and basically normal with a core body temperature of 33.4°C and warming. But I was stable.

As I said, I have seen many styles of recovery and I developed my own preferred method. I also realised that there were other experienced ice swimmers developing their own recovery process styles. I realised, too, that some like the hot wet towels and some don't. Some like the sauna and some hate it. Many don't like a warm shower, however, I do. Some like to lie down under blankets, but I hate it! Some like to walk and some like to sit.

My Recovery Method

I like to be able to walk out of every swim, unassisted. I always say, "I like to finish an Ice Swim with dignity, that means I haven't gone way too far." I can't say I always managed that, but I certainly tried. I don't like to be handled, pulled or pushed. I feel very 'brittle' when I come out and experience has shown me that I can get injured easily in the recovery regardless of the fact that I don't recall pain or the incident. I am very well aware that my control is lacking, but the effort to walk and manage my recovery taught me to recover very fast over time. I don't confuse recovery with rewarming, which I know may take much longer.

I Trained in any conditions, Camps Bay Gale force wind

I like to have my goggles and cap off as soon as possible, gently, but off. I am very aware of that pressure on my face and head. I need it to go away and I want to dry my head and face. It gives me a good level of comfort. I like to manage my recovery so I can remain active. I am aware that one of my main strengths in the ice is my body's ability to generate heat while swimming, a good amount of heat. When I stop swimming, I try and continue that process and slowly stop. I just like to remain active. Nothing radical, no running, jumping etc....just to be active. I walk around and move in any way I feel comfortable with.

I like to get to a warm place as soon as possible too (I assume this is very normal) and I like to start the rewarming process. I don't like to lie down. I tried it twice and it created chaos in my brain. I think that the horizontal position so soon in the after-drop period brings icy blood to my brain and as mentioned before, it seems to cause a sudden rapid drop of brain core temperature, which throws me into an orbital space odyssey 2001 trip.

So, I simply refuse to lie down unless I am in a medical situation that requires it. Once the after-drop roller coaster ride starts, I prefer to sit down and focus. I continue the rewarming process while keeping my eyes open at all times. I want to know where I am, what is going on and to watch the ride so I can see the end. I allow for a shiver, but I try and control my breathing and relax. Severe shivers have caused me some serious muscle cramps and can derail me from the ride back into space.

I stay away from a jacuzzi for a while. Again, the reason is that water conducts heat 30 times faster than the air and that induces rewarming too quickly, ejecting me into the dark space again. I do love the jacuzzi, but only once the after-drop process shifts into pure rewarming. I don't mind the hot wet towel although I know some who don't like it at all.

I personally prefer a dry sauna for a while and then a shower. Yes, shower! I am generally ready for the shower after around ten minutes from the swim ends. I can sit or stand, sometimes with some help. I usually start the shower with lukewarm water, probably around 25°C. I take the temperature up slowly as I feel the need to rewarm. I make sure my head is out of the water for quite some time. Again, the reason, I assume, is to allow the core temperature of my brain to adjust slowly. I will put my head under the water when I know I have turned the corner. I can indulge in the shower for hours, but I usually stay for five to ten minutes after which I dry myself and dress.

Again, I have learnt a lot over time. My recovery after a 1 km ice swim is very quick, even if the water temperature is around zero. I know I haven't been in the water for too long, so the after-drop will be a very short ride. I hold tight for a couple of minutes and then it's gone, rewarming taking its time most times. In mile swims, my recovery is harder and longer. However, I have had great 2–3°C mile swims and tough 4–5°C swims. The same applies to recovery. I always brace myself for a serious ride and then surprise myself.

My conclusion regarding the medical recovery procedures is that we follow the professional experience and trust it. However, when it comes to a personal process, we need to develop our best individual method. One needs to identify what works best for you and develop on it. We have the ability to handle pain and misery well and some maybe are even addicted to it in some bizarre way, like all extreme and ultra-endurance athletes. But we handle it differently. Stroke is about technique, recovery has some rules and the rest is individual.

A few extra tips. Never recover on your own. Always have someone observing your recovery in case you get into trouble. As to the eyes! If you watch a swimmer's eyes in recovery, the eyes look right through you. They look at nowhere. Their look is inward that is why it looks like they are seeing right through you. The eyes are like a screen sending messages if you care to watch.

Once the eyes start engaging and look outwards and the swimmer starts to respond to actions in front of them, acknowledge conversation and questions, the swimmer is coming back from his/her internal battle. When the eyes smile, the swimmer is back! But they will still be cold inside.

We have all learnt a lot in the past several years. We all are looking to push more, further, always exploring. That is the beautiful part of the ice, so don't hold your knowledge and experiences. Share them, teach your learnings and it may just save someone some pain and risk and possibly save someone's life one day.

Be safe and never be scared to dare…

Chapter 12
Life with Celiac Disease

It was early 2000 and a lot has happened in my personal life. I had just split up with my first wife after 20 years since we met. We had three young kids and needless to say, life was very testing.

I made sure I was always five minutes away from my kids regardless that was my rule of thumb, but even seeing them every weekend and dealing with the consequences of reality was a tough toll. At the same time, things at Cadiz took a tough turn as well. The euphoria and honeymoon of listing on the stock exchange, so many new faces and the success that followed placed us in a very tough place. Egos had started to soar and we faced serious inside politics. My health was already heading downhill as I was losing weight rapidly and my immune system was starting to fail.

But in typical 'man style' when the going gets tough, we toughen up. It wasn't though, all about, just about manning up. It was looking after my body, which in many ways, as healthy and active as I had been, I had very little regard for my body. Everything went in but when very little to almost nothing stayed in, I realised I may be in trouble. I was 20kg lighter than now and I am not at 80kg, that's 25% of my body weight.

Celiac, as far as we know, is a hereditary disease passed on through genetics. You can go through life never really worrying about it, but it usually gets triggered by certain events. Traumatic events are one of those events and I had just had an event that erupted like a volcano in more ways than one.

What is Celiac Disease?

*'Celiac disease is a serious autoimmune disorder that can occur in genetically predisposed people, where the ingestion of gluten leads to damage

to the small intestine. It is estimated to affect one in 100 people worldwide. Two and one-half million Americans are undiagnosed and are at risk for long-term health complications.'

What are the Long-Term Effects?

*'Celiac disease can develop at any age and generally, it started after people started eating foods or medicines that contained gluten. Left untreated, celiac disease can lead to additional serious health problems. These include the development of other autoimmune disorders like Type I diabetes and multiple sclerosis (MS), anaemia, osteoporosis, infertility and miscarriage, neurological conditions like epilepsy and migraines, short stature and intestinal cancers.'

Sounds scary, right? Not as scared as I was when I found out. It is still a very unknown disease despite the fact that it affects one in 100 people worldwide. With a population of 8 billion people, 1% have the disease, which is around 80 million people. Yet, very few know about it. The recent trend of gluten-free products helped a lot to find these food sources, but at the same time created a perception that it was all about your diet trend rather than a serious medical condition.

Once thought to afflict mostly Caucasians, celiac disease has become cosmopolitan. It appears with higher than expected frequency in parts of North Africa, the Middle East and Asia. In India, it poses a growing public health concern. Meanwhile, in North America, evidence suggests patients and doctors need to stop assuming that it affects primarily white people from Western Europe. A new study of celiac disease and ethnicity in the United States emphasises its diversity. Researchers found that people from the Punjab region of northern India were more likely than other Americans to have the disease while the prevalence is also high among people of Jewish and Middle Eastern backgrounds. (Published 6 October 2016 by Van Waffle.)

*References – Medical Encyclopaedia.

I decide to write a small chapter on this for two reasons. First, it has changed my life and is still a major factor affecting my lifestyle. Second, to create awareness. There are millions out there, just like me, who discovered it at the age of 43 after losing 20 kg and thinking that I probably had cancer or worse, cancer having similar symptoms. There are so many people with various degrees of autoimmune disorders which manifest themselves in a very painful way. But it can be treated, not cured, mind you. It calls for a massive change in lifestyle and nutrition and straying away from that lifestyle can be very painful.

I am not going to bore you with technical details, but I will tell you how it entered my life and how it affected my life in a most dramatic way. Maybe it will help you if you have an autoimmune disorder or it can help you understand others who live with this all their life, just like a disability, but manage it.

I never liked pastry, pasta, pizza and other very rich foods, basically foods with loads of gluten. It simply made me feel sick, so I avoided it. I did love fresh bread and sometimes a slice of cake, but usually, I avoided it. The beer tasted great and still does, but it always hurt me, so it was an endurance process.

In early 2000, when I realised I couldn't keep a beer in for more than one minute, I decided it was time to see a doctor. It was a quick diagnosis. I had never heard of it before and there was no cure, just a lifestyle adjustment. I realised it was very simple; I either changed my lifestyle dramatically or it would kill me. I understood and did just that. Even right now, as I write this chapter in a coffee shop, ordering some food, the waitress has no idea what gluten is let alone what celiac disease is. Even though the menu is marked and the chef should know.

Ninety-five per cent of processed foods contain gluten. It is mostly wheat and it is a great binder of foods, good for preservatives and cheap thickening. If it wasn't for plenty of new gluten-free products, a person with celiac disease simply couldn't eat out anymore. Kids with celiac disease could only eat food made at home by their parents, nothing else! Can you imagine what it is like as a child not to be allowed to touch any food, any nice sweet ever? Most ice cream, chocolates and other sweets contain gluten. If you want to be on the safe side, simply don't ever touch anything with gluten. It will hurt you. Not immediately and not always, but there is no cure. Even if you felt great for years, it is always there awaiting your gluten intake to inflame your insides.

It has certainly changed my life and I am not very disciplined when it comes to gluten intake, so every now and then I stray and receive a serious wake-up call. You can spend 80% of your life with stomach cramps and pains, sometimes so debilitating that you simply can't be sociable or in public. However, like any disability, you adapt. It becomes normal to you and although it can be very frustrating at times, you put it in perspective and realise that it is not so bad and that it actually can lead you to a significantly healthier lifestyle.

Due to my strong head personality, when presented with a serious problem, I instinctively search for a solution or an opportunity. Simple physics, action-reaction or law of conservation of energy, nothing is without a reason, nothing is pure wastage and every problem presents an opportunity. Celiac disease has changed my health dramatically. I started eating simple and healthy. I avoided rich foods and preservatives. I gained weight and suddenly I could handle the cold water much better. I even considered that the habitual stomach pains allowed me to handle the tight stomach muscles at ice swimming better. It has certainly taught me a lot about pain management, which is an integral part of ice swimming, cold water swimming and most extreme endurance sports.

Before I realised I was Celiac – skin and bones

Celiac disease is certainly no fun. Travelling the world has become quite complex with having to search for food I can eat. Going out can be a nightmare. Many times, it imposes on my company who have to accommodate my choice of foods or restaurants. Ordering is always a complicated task and adds some language barrier to that mix and you are simply #$%$@. It certainly has thought me a lot of tolerance, which is still a never-ending learning curve for me.

Although it is not a visible disability, it is a form of handicap and it requires serious adjustment, which has taught me huge respect for people with serious disabilities. Respect for those who have the patience and perseverance to continue and make the best of their life. I've met a few of them in my extreme sports life. I am always very curious about their disabilities and how they handle life and adapt and many times flourish. It fascinates me and it gives me huge strength and inspiration. It puts my adversities into perspective and it shows me that in every adversity, you can find strength.

It is not easy and sometimes depressing and almost debilitating, but when you manage to overcome that, you are certainly stronger, taller and more tolerant of life.

Chapter 13
Round Cape Peninsula Swim

It was my swim interval and it was pitch dark. We were around a mile or more offshore outside Kommetjie. I recall seeing the lighthouse in the distance as it was the only reference to how far out we were. The time was 1 am, the water was 11°C and we were certainly in great white territory. Offshore, middle of the night…swimming, I mean, why not?

I couldn't swim close to the big yacht, which was our support boat, so I had to dive in and align a few meters away from the yacht. I had a small light stick attached to my swimming costume and I swam towards the support kayak, which was marked with another light stick. The kayaker mentioned that there was a lot of movement in the water and it looked like dolphins. With that sobering thought in my mind, I saw dozens of black shadows sprinting around under me. I forced my mind to agree that these were Dolphins. There I was – wearing a standard swimming costume, one silicon cap and a pair of goggles.

The water was icy and I was still shivering from my last swim. The intended shift was 30 minutes each, however, a few of the swimmers were in mild hypothermia and were struggling to stay in the water for more than 10-20 minutes. There were those hardcore die-hards who decided we would do 40 minutes at a time to allow the others more time to recover. We were such nice guys! Today, if I had to have taken on that challenge, it wouldn't have worried me at all; the dark, the dolphins, and the possibility of sharks or the ice had numbed my brain. But back then, I was petrified. When I asked the kayaker if it was really dolphins or just others swimming with me, he thought it was quite funny until I made it clear to him that that kind of sense of humour would place him in the water with me.

The one wonderful thing about the icy cold water is that it focuses you on its intensity. You can't ignore it. You let it in but never let it take over. It requires serious concentration and focus. There was no time for sharks or other moving parts in the water. I had to swim.

It was 11°C and pitch dark. And all I could see were a few dots of lights. I hoped they would stay close by. Forty minutes passed quickly.

***

It was early 2004 and I somehow had heard about a group of young six students from The University of Cape Town wanting to swim around the Cape Peninsula in a non-stop relay. The swim was to start from Kalk Bay, a small fishing harbour in the massive False Bay, part of the Indian Ocean side of the Peninsula. The route around Cape Point to the waterfront in Cape Town was around 100 km. I recognised one of the swimmers, Sarah, and I contacted her to find out if an old geezer like me would be allowed to join the youth of 20-something-year-olds in their epic adventure.

I had started to build up a name for myself as the guy who swam open water and cold water swims, but in my books, I was as inexperienced as they were. Sure, I did have age, possible wisdom and a fearless mindset, which helped a lot. I only found out later on that they had been concerned that I was bringing in a vast amount of experience and wisdom; they were essentially a bit intimidated. It was a typical life twist; expectations versus reality.

To my delight the young group accepted me and we spent a few weeks in preparation for the swim and training. They were a great bunch, full of youth and excitement and I felt very welcome although I certainly felt a tad out of place. Nevertheless, I later got to know some of them better and to this day remain friends for life.

The day finally arrived. We met at 2 am at Kalk Bay Harbour. The harbour is home to a few big seals feeding off the fishing boats and swimming in False Bay was still relatively safe then. It was soon after that swim that the great white population grew and shark spotting was recorded daily. Following several shark attacks, all swimming events in False Bay were sadly cancelled and they still are many years later.

Paul was the first swimmer. He dived into the pitch-black water from the far harbour wall and started our adventure. It was 4 am by that stage. The water in False Bay is usually warmer than the other side of the peninsula as it's the Indian Ocean. I recall a temperature of around 16°C. It was summer, so although the air was chilly, there was an early dusk morning chill. I was swimming second and dived in around 2 km offshore from Fish Hoek, later to be known as a daily great white feeding route. It was epic and I swam into the sunrise to my left, shining on the coastline on my right. I would breathe to the right so as it was one of those swims that provided non-stop beautiful coastline entertainment.

During the day, the swims and rests were just beautiful. It is one of the most picturesque coastlines in the world and there we were swimming along with it. The changeover went smoothly and we swam 30 minutes at a time with three hours of rest with plenty of time to eat, chirp and catch some sun. We were moving at a nice pace and we approached Cape Point, a very dangerous place if you catch it in a bad mood, which happens often there with the southeaster wind. As we approached the point, we all decided to dive in and swim around the point together. The sea was beautiful with some swell around 14°C and the sun was starting to sink. We knew that the real part was coming still.

As the sun disappeared, so did the balmy water temperature. We turned into Cape Point, part of the Atlantic Ocean and the water temperature started to drop drastically and finally settled around 11°C. Along with the water drop, the air temperature dropped as well. We were far out at sea, literally at the end of the world, swimming in the dark. Some of us started to take serious strain and one of the swimmers was already out due to seasickness. Oddly, our support person was also down with seasickness. I was absolutely fine though and for whatever reason, I never get seasick. In fact, the fresh air and the sea invigorate me, making me feel alive and super hungry.

It wasn't long, though, before the entire team started to take the strain. Some couldn't spend much time in the water so the others tried to compensate for it. Yet, doing the extra time with shorter rests made the recovery very difficult. We had a sleeping bag with hot air pumped into it and when you had finished your swim, you could jump in until the next swimmer got out to claim it.

Sleep was impossible although I recall a few bodies scattered around covered with heaps of blankets all over the deck. We worked as a team. The youngsters impressed me so much. There was no ego, just helping each other to get through the freezing wet night. There were lots of passing hot soup around, drinking chocolate and offering general support. It was very important to know that you were not alone and you were in caring safe hands. That is critical in the cold.

It was around 2 or 3 am when I became semi-delirious from cold and fatigue. I remember it was Julz's turn to swim and Lewis (Pugh), who was doing the list couldn't find her. He finally did find her fast asleep, still shivering though from her last swim. She woke up to the shouts of, "Next swimmer…get ready." As a swimmer, it was important that your shift was watched and the next swimmer was there on time. It was an immense comfort to know that while you were swimming, the next swimmer was getting ready to take your place.

I was lying in front of Lewis in a warm sleeping bag, still shivering from my last swim and Lewis looked at me. We both realised that Julz, now in tears, frozen and fatigued, was in no state to jump back in and swim in 11°C of pitch-dark water. I looked back at Lewis knowing what was coming. Diligently, I got out of the warm fuzzy womb state I was in and nodded. I dived in and started another 40 minutes of swimming in the dark. The cold was my friend. It focused me. The darkness was also my friend as it allowed my mind to wonder. And so, I zoned out and soon it was all over.

There is nothing more beautiful than a sunrise whilst out there in the cold sea. And with a nice cup of coffee in hand, it makes one feel quite special. We were just outside of Hout Bay, my home at the time, and the gang was slowly defrosting cheerfully and a sense of humour re-emerged from a deep quiet sleep. With the warm sun on your back, you can think about your distant cold-water swim with a whimsical air.

We were scheduled to swim into the V&A at 12 pm and we had a huge reception awaiting us. The youngsters had done a marvellous job organising the swim. 30 hours and 100 km after the 4 am departure, we arrived at the waterfront.

We stopped for two hours before the waterfront so that we would arrive exactly at noon. At around 500 m before the V&A waterfront, we all dived in, welcomed by a few well-fed seals and thousands of people standing in every possible restaurant and on all the walls cheering us on. It was an amazing sight. We were waterlogged, tired but also floating in the air with a huge sense of achievement.

We had done it!

Was it tough? Difficult to say really. It was certainly challenging and at times, we each had to dig deep, however, the team spirit made it very possible and clocked down to another great adventure.

Swimming in False Bay, home of the Great White Sharks, sunrise

I later came back to swim Cape Point for an 8 km swims another three times. I still considered it one of the most epic swims out there. You are at the end of Africa, out in the dark ocean, where the Cape Agulhas and Benguela Current meet and the water temperature can change around 4°C in just a few meters. Yes, some of the world's great white sharks are also known to enjoy this epic swim, but all is fine as long as they don't get in our space.

Years later, I decided to do the swim from Simon's Town to Muizenberg, a 10 km swim that was stopped due to shark sightings. I was determined and attempted it about 14 years later. It was a summer swim due to the weather conditions and I followed the shark spotter website every day prior to the swim date. No sightings for two weeks. So, I called the swim and off we went. I swam alone with two boats around me and it was a beautiful swim. We arrived at Muizenberg, but my boats had to stay behind the waves line around 200 m from shore. It was at the surfers' corner where all the shark's attacks had occurred. It would be a sprint; I had no choice although I don't sprint. I managed to get to shore fully intact and walked out in my speedo to everyone's amusement. A few paces up to my car, I dug my car key out from under a nearby rock and drove off. It was epic.

The next day, I checked the shark spotter site and discovered that they had forgotten to update the site for two weeks. It was now up to date though and two sightings had occurred the day before I swam, three the day after, and none the day I swam though. All great white sharks. Well, needless to say, thank God they forgot to update it or I may never have swum.

Chapter 14
The Orange River 2000 km Challenge

I barely slept that night. My tiny tent was perched on the edge of the cliff next to the Orange River at the Lesotho border. It was around 4 am with 30 minutes to sunrise. I woke up to this muffled singing, "Happy birthday, Ram…"

I opened my eyes and all I could see was a circle of dark shadows around my tent. The wind was howling and it was freezing cold. It was my birthday, on the Orange River, again, and I was given the first swimming slot today as we started another 500–600 km swimming adventure on the Orange River.

Swimming the Orange River

I woke up, crawled outside and 30 minutes later, after preparing our kayaks, gear and food for a 15-hour day on the river, I dived in to start our day. The Orange River gushes down from the mountain of Lesotho, where its origin is up in the Drakensberg. The river was full and flowing at three knots an hour, thick brown from the mud, it picks up along the mountain. The water was so thick with mud, you could taste the soil every time you took a breath.

Our swimming costume didn't survive on this trip.

It was my second birthday on the river. For the other one, I had to swim with a pirate patch and a wee sword attached to my goggles. I was away from my family, but I was in my element with friends, in the water, swimming…it is just a date. I celebrated again when I got home.

The Orange River (from Afrikaans/Dutch *oranjerivier*) is the longest river in South Africa and the Orange River Basin extends extensively into Namibia and Botswana to the north. It rises in the Drakensberg mountains in Lesotho, flowing westwards through South Africa to the Atlantic Ocean. The river forms part of the international borders between South Africa and Namibia and between South Africa and Lesotho, as well as several provincial borders within South Africa. Except for Upington, it does not pass through any major cities. The Orange River plays an important role in the South African economy by providing water for irrigation and hydroelectric power. The river was named by Robert Jacob Gordon after the Dutch Royal House. Other names include Gariep River (used by the Khoi people), Groote River or Senqu River (used in Lesotho). (Wikipedia)

The Orange River rises in the Drakensberg mountains along the border between South Africa and Lesotho about 193 km (120 mi) west of the Indian Ocean and at an altitude of over 3,000 m. The extremity of the Orange River inside Lesotho is known as the Senqu. Parts of the Senqu River freeze in winter because of the high altitude there. This creates droughts downstream, which mainly affect goat and cattle production.

The Orange River then runs westward through South Africa forming the south-western boundary of the Free State province. In this section, the river flows first into the Gariep Dam (the largest in the country) and later into the Vanderkloof Dam. From the border of Lesotho to below the Van der Kloof Dam, the river bed is deeply incised. Further downstream, the land is flatter and the river is used extensively for irrigation.

At the western point of the Free State, southwest of Kimberley, the Orange River meets with its main tributary, the Vaal River, which itself forms much of the northern border of the province. From here, the river flows further westward through the arid wilderness of the southern Kalahari Region and Namaqualand in the Northern Cape Province to meet with Namibia at 20°E longitude. From here, it flows westward for 550 km forming the international border between the province and Namibia's Karas Region. On the border, the river passes the town of Vioolsdrif, the main border post between South Africa and Namibia.

In the last 800 km (500 mi) of its course, the Orange River receives many intermittent streams and several large wadis lead into it. In this section, the Namib Desert terminates on the north bank of the river, so under normal circumstances, the volume of water added by these tributaries is negligible. Here, the bed of the river is once again deeply incised. The Augrabies Falls are located on this section of the Orange River, where the river descends 122 m (400 ft) in a course of 26 km (16 mi).

The Orange River empties into the Atlantic Ocean between the small towns of Oranjemund (meaning 'orange mouth') in Namibia and Alexander Bay in South Africa about equidistant between Walvis Bay and Cape Town. Some 33 km (21 mi) from its mouth, it is completely obstructed by rapids and sand bars and is generally not navigable for long stretches.

The river has a total length of 2,200 km (1,400 mi).

The Orange River swim was the beginning of my swimming adventures. It started in 2003 one day at Constantia Gym after a swim session. Andrew asked me if I'm keen to swim the South African length of the Orange River around 2000 km in a relay. I paused for a second, looked at him and said, "I'm in." I didn't ask for details, dates, costs or any specifics. He knocked on a door, which was raring to burst open for a while. That was also the start of a great friendship that led to many adventures and new friends.

Kayaking

The actual adventure took us four years. We were all ordinary men and women who had day jobs and a family, so we couldn't just disappear for a month, so we decided to break it into four trips around 500 km each leg. Although it was Andrew's vision and dream born from Martin Strel's swim of the Mississippi, I ended up rolling my sleeves and helping him as much as needed, mind, matter and financially.

The drill was to cover as much distance per day from dawn to dusk, which at times was over 15 hours a day. We decided to do a relay with kayaks and one swimmer in the water at all times. We started with four kayaks on the first trip and went down to three kayaks for the rest of the trips. We used Andrew Kellett Gravity Adventures as our expedition and river guides and their kayaks. Two per kayak. We covered between 40 km to 80 km a day depending on the river flow. We swam 20 minutes at a time with a hi-five change over in the water. It gave us a good rest on the kayak, but many times swimming was actually easier than kayaking. Especially when we hit a strong headwind in the afternoon rowing against waves and chops. On average, we covered around 10 km of swimming per day and around 50 km of kayaking. We were very fit at the end of each leg.

The legs of the swim were decided according to dates availability and river flow and temperature at the time.

1. Orange River 1: Onseepkans to Orange River mouth
2. Orange River 2: Telle Bridge (your birthday) to Hopetown
3. Orange River 3: Hopetown to Upington
4. Orange River 4: Upington to Onseepkans

Each one of these mini-adventures was a different story and could have been a different book if we had put pen to paper at the time. It is hard to remember the daily details of each trip but I still remember that none of them was easy and there were blood, sweat and tears in each one of them.

Looking back at the first leg, we all could swim, some faster and some stronger. We all knew the basics of rowing but none of us spent significant time rowing before, especially down some roaring white waters. We didn't really know what to expect, the hype around our adventure was quite dramatic, which is exactly what I don't like. Few said we are mad, which I like and few said we will never succeed, which I ignored. But like us, most had no idea what we are heading into.

There are two basic things one needs to know in an expedition. One, look after your equipment and two, look after your body. Needless to say, we failed in both. We got much better on the second trip, but the first trip tested us deeply. When you spend 15 hours on a river, swimming and paddling, you need to have a few extras of each one of the critical items you use. The river demands its tax and regardless of how much experienced you are, the river demands its payment.

I think I lost just about everything I could lose on the first trip. I even lost a life jacket! How on earth does one lose a life jacket in the water? Well, add white waters gushing down at 20 knots with a carefully scattered variety of rocks and one roll and the life jacket, which was supposed to be secured on the kayak, disappeared. It never floated, it actually got dumped under the massive white water and ended up stuck under the rocks. Luckily, I wasn't attached to it this time. The rest? Sunglasses, hats, food, camera, and basically everything I had and forgot to secure properly has simply vanished in the water.

I developed a speciality, which earned me a fine 'prize' at the end – to place the kayak on top of a rock in the middle of the white water rapidly. Not only did I manage to get on the rock, but I also managed to do it in such a way that the gushing water wrapped the kayak on the rock and made it almost impossible to rescue. Luckily, those kayaks were flexible plastic and we always managed to unwrap them at some stage with 'limited' damage. I also managed to break the kayak rudder or back skeg on the first day. This part is crucial in helping you to keep the kayak moving in a straight line. I spent the rest of the first trip trying to keep a straight line. Some say it still affects my swimming to date.

One of the elements I missed completely was nutrition. We had food and lots of energy bars and water. We had a very early breakfast, basic and tasteless, but the coffee bridged the gaps (tasteless as well). We packed for the day, knowing that the next meal or the only real meal for the day will come later in the evening by the fireplace.

Although we worked hard, we had a lot of downtime while rowing on the kayak. We had some seriously challenging times but as a whole, it wasn't hard all the time, it was hard and very hard at times, but we were physically active 15 hours a day, almost non-stop. I snacked on a few bananas, a boiled egg and an occasional energy bar. By the end of day three, I was shivering and feeling very weak. I was very worried that I caught something until Sheryl, a seasoned ironman (woman), reprimanded me on my nutrition.

One big meal at the end of the day simply doesn't do it. I got into the routine of eating something every hour and an energy bar after every swim. The body was burning lots of calories all the time, the heat, the sun and the water demanded their price and I needed to eat and drink all the time. I learnt a lot since, but the deceiving part was not just ignorance, it was the fact that we were not in an ironman race, we were swimming and paddling, with high spirits and amazing scenery. We didn't see ourselves on a serious expedition until it depleted us.

The other part that nearly brought us to a halt was our bodies. We spent 15 hours a day in and out of the water. The air temperature varied to highs of 51°C midday and quite chilly at night. It was summer but we were on the border of the Namibian Desert. Somehow, a foot fungus appeared and started to spread among us. We had several debates as to the source. We all used to train a lot at the gym pool those days and it probably found someone's toe to hitch a ride to the Orange River. Slowly but surely, that fungus started to spread from toes to the foot, to leg and from one to the other. I'll spare you the details, expeditions have many unpleasant and mostly undignified times. When you are in there, all the inhibitions are gone, and you are focused on survival.

The fungus ate into our toes and feet so deeply it was unbearable. The fact that we had to swim and get dry as an ongoing routine kept our wounds wet and dry to the extent that we developed deep raw cracks between our toes and on our feet. It was extremely painful. Think about dry lips, cracking an inch deep into your lips. We ended up filling every possible crack on our feet with Vaseline. It became a ritual after every swimming interval. Quickly before the sun-dried our skin, we pumped Vaseline into our agonised crack, on our feet. The expedition logistics managed to find iodine in some remote town and we spent the evenings taking turns soaking our feet in a bucket full of iodine. Vivienne, one of the swimmers, was a pharmacist. I asked her at the height of my agony with a few days to go, "What can I do?"

She replied, "Nothing, just deal with it." Little harsh but a pearl of wisdom in expeditions like that. I wasn't in any real danger, just excorticating agony and discomfort. I simply had to treat it and ride it until we get home and recover. Many times, later, in different hard situations, I reminded myself to check if I am in any real danger when the answer was no, I knew 'head down' and get on with it. All those exotic adventures have a price tag, which many times are much dearer than the financial one. If you are attracted to the glory rather than the experience, all I can say is good luck, fasten your seat belt, and a ride of your lifetime is heading your way.

The days on the river went rather slow. An expedition is many times about a daily tedious routine that allows you to cover distances safely. We had lots of fun; I can't deny that. We chirped, sang, argued and at times went all very, very quiet, especially when the day dragged and dragged and a sense of humour left us alone and the fatigue settled in. We saw various animals in and out of the water. Swimming with a bloated, large, dead antelope or kudu floating by or a big swimming cobra that was crossing the swimming route while Andrew was swimming. It looked like both are heading into a collision path unaware of each other. I decided to keep it that way and hope they will just miss each other. I knew if I shout at Andrew 'watch out for the swimming black cobra heading your way...' will cause such a reaction that will guarantee collusion. I also knew that trying to distract the cobra may entice it to change direction towards Andrew. So, we just watched…and it was soon over, rather close though.

On one of the days, the sun was heading down and we were far from our landing spot. The river is not very accessible in many places which forced the logistics vehicle to travel vast distances by land and back to get to our spot. On that day, the truck had to cover around 700 km by land to be able to reach our overnight spot, which was around 80 km down the river. The expedition leader said we have little far to go but had no clarity as to where.

Sun was going down and the river was flowing. Morale was very low and fatigue was taking over. I decided to step in and told everyone to get on the kayak. We can't swim in the dark with rapids. No objections, we started to paddle in the dark. When we went through quiet flat spots, it was so surreal and beautiful. In the African desert, there are no lights, just stars and water. We went through two large white water sections. It was also surreal and seriously scary. The benefit of white water is that they create some glow in the dark and give you some sense of where they are.

I was on the kayak with Cheryl and masterfully managed to wrap our kayak around a massive rock in the middle of the rapids. Emotions were rather high, but we managed to unwrap ourselves and down the rapid, we went. Around 9 pm, after a very long day with a 3 am wake up, we suddenly turned a corner and saw our logistic vehicle and a fireplace. We could smell food. It was an amazing sensation. And suddenly 20 minutes later, we were all around the fire with beers and the tears and agony of the day disappeared. Well, until the next day.

As we got closer to the river mouth by the Atlantic Sea, two things happened. The water temperature started to drop from 32°C to as low as 14°C. The other was the afternoon wind. The thermal created from the sea and land temperatures raised a punching headwind from around 2 pm to sunset. The river winds around like a snake and suddenly, as we turned a corner, we were hit by a 30 knots headwind, a big chop and basically a wall! Our kayaks were not suited for such a headwind and it became almost impossible to move forward. The chop threw the kayak sideways and trying to keep it straight dead ahead was a battle.

The main challenge was for the kayak with a swimmer in the water. It was left for one person to paddle with no weight in the front, which nearly caused the kayak to be airborne. Swimming was also a serious challenge, but we all knew waves and swimming in waves, so it was actually fun. It was very difficult for the kayak to keep up with the swimmer who was moving at around 2 km an hour anyways. What actually saved us was the fact that the river does snake around the desert looking for a route of least resistance. This broke our battle to manageable bite-size. We covered the distance very slowly, but we moved forward. In my mind, most 'impossible and bigger than life challenges can be conquered, slowly, if you manage a way to reduce them to small bite chunks and then take it one at a time…until it is behind you. In long-distance swims, we refer to this strategy as 'one feed at a time'.

The exhausted 1st Orange River swim team

The first leg was over. We poured into the Atlantic Ocean at around 13°C. It was refreshing but we were not acclimatised to it. There were some nice shore breaks and we all had fun. I suddenly realised I am being swept out to sea. I was in the middle of a strong rip tide alone. The thing about rip tides is that out on the beach when you see them, you know exactly what to do and how to go around them. But when it catches you unprepared while you are on top of the world after 11 days of gruelling expedition, it suddenly gets very scary.

We all spread around the beach and I realised, it is me and the rip. No one else. I was starting to panic, that was not on the Orange River expedition program. We have a huge party tonight and everyone was gathering with bottles of champagne on the beach. I somehow managed to swim around it and get back to the beach. No one noticed aside from, "Where is Ram…?" The champagne suddenly tasted twice as good.

Later on, in swimming, I got stuck in a much stronger rip tide and shore break several times. It is part of swimming in our oceans here. You get caught and suddenly it all goes pair shape in a second. Don't panic when you panic! Everyone panics a little, so when you realise you do, try and manage it…it can be the difference between life and death, as simple as that. I'm still working on it and still very much alive.

We came back again and again for another three years. Different team but the same core of people. Andrew, Cheryl and I are the only ones who managed to cover the entire river. Gavin missed a year and Hester missed two. Others just came for a year. Every section was different, but we learnt a lot. I was prepared. My nutrition, my equipment and I actually learnt how to skip these hostile rocks in the middle of the rapids. We had some hairy occasions, bumping head in the rapid under the water, seeing Cheryl stuck upside down in a rapid head under legs in the air, mostly tears and lots of laughter. The Orange River was an epic adventure. I decided I had enough of warm rivers, I prefer cold oceans and ice.

Chapter 15
The Robben Island Night Swim

The idea to do the infamous Robben Island to Blouberg crossing at night came to me following a recent visit to Robben Island.

A couple of months before the decision, a bunch of us from Cadiz Holdings went on a private Robben Island tour with our partners from Makana Trust. Makana is a trust set up by Mandela and a few others to benefit all the ex-political prisoners from Robben Island. After the tour, which was phenomenal, we took the ferry back to the waterfront. By that stage, the sun was going down and I was standing at the back of the ferry watching the waves, thinking about the usual swim route back to Blouberg. A thought popped into my head, *Wouldn't this be an interesting challenge to swim the route at night?* I mulled over it asking myself questions like, *What it would be like doing this swim? What would real challenges be? Would it be safe?* And so on.

I tested the idea with a few friends and the only response I received was a strange look and a comment, "You must be mad!" It wasn't the first time I had received that comment though through my many years on this good earth. Anyway, I went through the possible dangers and challenges that the swim could bring and concluded that if all safety measures were taken, it would be possible. The real challenge would be in my mind. At the end of the day, the actual obstacle in life, when you want to achieve something, is ourselves. So, I set out to do some research first.

The first and most fearful issue was 'Bruce' and his friends (Repeat after me, a fish is our friend, not a food), a *Finding Nemo* memory. I spoke to a few other people and they remarked that sharks are nocturnal animals and they do prefer feeding at night. Great! Can't they go out drinking and develop some social life? I contacted Peter Bales and asked him about the shark shield we used for the around the Cape Point swim. He directed me to the website of the company manufacturing them (http://www.sharkshield.com). I read every single article, technical specification and testimonials there was to be found on this device.

They seemed to be factual and comprehensive. The shark shield was the solution it seemed, but I also read statements like, *It should be safe as long as you don't swim into the dangling electrical whip.* And, *It can cause severe discomfort.* Okay then!

Wonderful! The main obstacle had been eliminated, at least according to the book. I wondered, cynically, if sharks had access to the Internet. I then spoke to the company and also to Cape Long Distance Associations who assured me that I could borrow their device for the swim.

Robben Island Night swim

The next obstacle was the water temperature and the lack of visibility at night. During the day, you get the sun shining on your back and the air that you breathe is warm. At night, all you have is the moonlight and air temperature that can be colder than the water temperature, which makes every breath you take like ice to your lungs.

I decided to try and select a night after a cold front and a North Westerly wind had blown, which should warm the surface water. The following should be warm with little or no wind. As to the visibility, it should be a full moon, clear skies, no waves and no fog. It sounded perfect. But ordering this combination of weather in Cape Town was close to impossible. I realised that I needed to prioritise the conditions and go with the best-case scenario.

So, breaking it down, the water temperature was the most important factor and then came the flat sea and clear skies. I tried to find a partner to join me in my madness, but strange enough, my great idea was received very coldly by most. I put the idea in the back of my mind and continued with the cold water Sunday swims in Camps Bay and Fish Hoek. We usually swam every Sunday for 30–45 minutes in the sea and the temperature varied from 9°C degrees to a lukewarm 15°C.

And then something happened. I went to see the film *'Touching the Void'* and I was extremely impressed and inspired. If you haven't seen it, the film was about two young climbers, who decide to attempt the summit of Siula Grande in the Peruvian Andes. They go through some trials and tribulations, which I found most intriguing.

A week later, we had the annual Cape Long Distance Swimming Association medal award ceremony for all the loonies who swam in the sea.

The atmosphere at these events was always very friendly and humble. As mentioned, the real challenge for all of us is always ourselves. We were not there to prove anything to anyone or try to beat each other but rather to encourage and inspire each other to face our own fears and mental strength. It worked.

After the third Gin and Tonic, as one does, I started assembling the required info and team for my night swim. The team was extremely critical for a challenge like that. Basically, the team is responsible for your life. All the swimmer has to do is put his head down and swim. The team does the rest, which sounded like a fair deal to me. I got hold of Dantjie, a seasoned boatman with great experience in the sea. His boat had a GPS, lights and three engines, just in case. He wasn't at all excited about the prospect, but I managed to convince him that he would enjoy it and he actually believed me. Next on the list was a second. I called Lewis Pugh to second me and he agreed.

And so, we needed to decide on the most perfect night. There was a Wednesday evening with a full moon coming up and I looked at the weather report concluding that the following Friday night may be as close to perfect as we were going to get. And off we would go.

Now something to note: Never ask a fisherman for the water temperature. They will always give you a figure of around 6°C off the range, which for you, the swimmer, could mean the difference between bearable to ice-cold water. They usually think we are absolutely mad anyways.

The logistics were quite a story from landing rights on Robben Island at night to organising sea kayaks, to arranging a doctor for emergencies and to dropping us off in the ocean at 8 pm, not to mention sorting a pick up for us on Blouberg Big Bay beach at 1 am the Saturday morning.

So, Friday arrives and I take a call from Jill, a fellow swimmer, "Can I join you on the swim? Not officially, but just for fun." I said yes, however, in hindsight I learnt that when you plan a big swim for yourself, don't let last-minute dot com in. I should have said no, I didn't need 100% attention on my swim, it was risky enough. Nevertheless, I said, "sure."

I recommended some alternatives to her like going out and getting drunk on a Friday night as normal people do, but no, she wanted to train for the Gibraltar Strait swim and this was, for her, the perfect training session.

So, we met up at 8 pm at Oceana. Dantjie had the boat. François brought his Huey Tucker sea kayak. Lewis arranged the shark shield and Bryan (the doctor) pitched not really knowing what he had gotten himself into. The kids came with Nadine to say goodbye too. It was all quite surreal at that point. I knew it was a high-risk swim and I had taken it very seriously.

Lewis called us all for a safety briefing inside the club before we set off to Robben Island. It suddenly got all real and serious and all I wanted was a cosy fireplace, a glass of Lagavulin, 16 years old and good music. I already had good company. Lewis briefed us with military operation precision. He spoke about sharks, night vision, emergency procedures and comforted us that seals like to play with night swimmers so we mustn't get scared. I knew that a dark blob touching me in the middle of the swim would cause some serious discomfort to my heart though. I don't think Lewis knew I was a retired major from the 5 years in the active Israeli army and knew a little bit about planning and logistics of a risky operation. But I let him run the show, he loved it.

We got on the boat and headed towards Robben Island, trying to cover ourselves with blankets to retain maximum body temperature. The sea was getting rough and the southeaster offshore wind leftovers created some nice chops on the water. We finally arrived at the island. It was pitch dark, as you can imagine, and Lewis got into a wetsuit, dropped the sea kayak overboard and dived in.

Us swimmers stripped to our swimming costumes, a cap, a pair of goggles and nothing else. These were the rules from the Long Distance Swimming Association. In order to qualify, one had to start from the beach, so we greased ourselves, mainly against chafing, and dived in the water. The water was surprisingly warm at a balmy 16°C. We swam to the shore and jumped around for five minutes feeling quite freezing while Lewis was sorting out the shark shield. I wasn't stressed at all; however, I must have emptied my bladder about three times in those five minutes. I knew, though, that once we started swimming, this would become impossible as the vital organs shrink to an unmanageable size.

At 9:15 pm on that Friday evening, the swimming began. We dived in and started swimming. While the water was great at 16°C, the sea turbulence started to pick up straight into our faces. Lewis was battling with the sea kayak and we just had to go up and down while swallowing gallons of seawater. That was something that nothing can prepare you for unless you swam in it the night before. Tony Selmer mentioned something before about a relay swims in the English Channel in the dark. The fact that you can't see anything means you can't anticipate the water, so I decided to rely on my body sensors and switched off my eyesight. It helped a bit trying to synchronise with the motion of the waves. I felt fine and strong ploughing through the water.

What I didn't realise at the time was that we were advancing at a very slow pace. Before the swim, I decided to break the distance into four feeds every half an hour. After two hours, I figured it should be a home run. I had swum it before in two hours 12 minutes and another time in two hours 35 minutes, so I was working around those factors. For the first kilometre, there was a high concentration of phosphorus in the water. It was an amazing sight. In the pitch dark, all you could see was a trail of glowing bubbles following your stroke. It was almost tripping, but unfortunately, the cold creeping up on me reminded me that I was stuck in a huge body of water in the dead of the night on my way to Blouberg from Robben Island.

At one point, Jill was right behind me, the boat was on my left side and Lewis on my right. I was breathing to my right so I could keep my eyes on the sea kayak. After the first feed, a sip of lukewarm fast fuel, we carried on.

It was amazing how quickly one can lose warmth when one stops. Jill wasn't happy. She wasn't having fun. I felt the same too but put my head down and kept going. A little way on, I swam into huge kelp and stopped to warn Jill but ended up being too late. I heard the scream behind me, but all was well. It was just a mind game and I wasn't scared. I had already decided to just ignore any scary thoughts about sharks and just get on with it. As far as I was concerned, there wasn't much I could do if a great white shark, had decided to snack on me. I just put my faith in the instrument we had and focused on the swim.

The water temperature started to drop down to about 14°C. Cold water leaves a burning sensation on your skin and your skin surface goes quite numb and you feel it seeping inside you, literally creeping into your bones. Nevertheless, we carried on swimming. There was not much to see and very soon we started to lose the excitement of the whole adventure. It was definitely a mind game at that point and we needed to focus to not let our minds trick us.

I ran out of thoughts eventually. Sex entered my mind for a few minutes for want of something to think about and then the cold just took it far away. Now there are two ways to cope; park your mind somewhere and swim or count. I decided to count. We reached our second feed and then set off again.

By the time the third feed was due, I was getting very cold. I knew I was fine but felt extremely unpleasant. Thankfully, the water had calmed down somewhat and this made the swim easier, but my arms were getting tired. The skipper informed us that we had swum 3.2 km. I couldn't believe it. That meant two more hours of swimming. However, Lewis shouted, "One hour to go!" it's the only time you are allowed to lie, tell the swimmer it's almost there even if there are a few hours left.

So, we carried on swimming. Suddenly, Jill starts to shout and I can feel I am being stung. I know the familiar blue bottles sting which I had experienced from the around Cape Point swim. There was nothing we could do but just accelerate and try to get out of their space. How rude of us to disturb their Friday night, lol. I received a few little stings but Jill had a few nice big ones on her legs. Luckily, it was so cold that you feel nothing aside from the cold, of course.

My arms were getting tired by that stage and I felt that I didn't have too much left in them.

The fourth feed saw the skipper shouting, "Halfway!"

I nearly broke down. Halfway? I had planned to slide home after the fourth feed. I hadn't budgeted for this to happen and my mind was beginning to give up on me. We were both very cold at that stage, but I shouted, "Let's go!" and put my head down to swim again. I stopped caring about time or distance and just swam. But after a time, my mind started to conjure up images of sharks and I started thinking to myself, *How stupid can you be, Ram? What happens if you do get snacked by a shark?* For about 20 minutes I fought these thoughts and finally managed to get them out of my mind and started counting again.

I really had nothing left in my arms. Every time I tried to take a strong stroke, my shoulders and arms went on strike. So, I just took long strokes, which didn't take too much effort but created a consistent pace. I knew we were slowing down and a fleeting thought past through my mind that a shark should just end this miserable and stupid adventure. I was very cold and I tested my fingers for hyperthermia but knew I was okay. The rest of the swim was quite blurry. I remember feeding more and just putting my head down to count. I knew that with around 1000 strokes I would have covered a good distance, so I did that. I did allow myself a few seconds of self-pity but kept going.

A little later, I saw the guys on the boat flashing the light at the beach, but the beach didn't seem to be getting any closer. I just didn't care anymore. Head down, swim and count. Luckily, all bad things do come to an end. I even planned out my announcement of retiring from this insane cold water swimming but also wondered how long it would take me to forget this and think about the next swim.

I recall Lewis shouting a few times as we were starting to wander off and nearly got taken by the speedboat. Lewis had warned us upfront about an encounter with the propeller. I had no idea what time it was or how long we had been in the water, but suddenly, the most beautiful thing in the world appeared in front of my eyes – Big Bay rocks. A huge dark silhouette of the rocks formed just ahead of us. I knew from previous swims that we are almost home. A few hundred metres and we would be done.

I have seen swimmers' minds give up at that stage and if you let your mind loose for a second, you are gone. Lewis navigated us around the rocks. The swell was quite high but we just kept swimming and swimming. Then, as if by a miracle, I could stand. I tried to walk, but my legs were not listening to me. I can't remember much once we landed on the beach. I do remember, though, Robbie covering me with blankets and clothes and Hester, Patrick and François congratulating us. I remember seeing Kaitlin, my daughter, and wondering how she had arrived there.

Apparently, Lewis had come first out of the water in his sea kayak, screamed and ran back into the waves. Nadine had a panic attack thinking the worst, but Lewis had just been excited. Patrick pushed a bottle of Bells into my frozen hands and boy, did it feel good running down my throat.

I crawled into the car with Jill and we both had some coffee trying to warm up against the car heater. As I sat there, I couldn't comprehend how tired I was. It had taken us exactly three hours and 50 minutes to complete, a whole hour and a half longer than I had anticipated. It was just after 1 am. But it was over.

First-ever Robben Island midnight swim done

Chapter 16
Kinneret, The Sea of Galilee – and a Swim for Peace

Kinneret is the Hebrew name for the Sea of Galilee. Its roots are from the word *'kinnor'* (pronounced key nor) which is the Hebrew word for violin. And the reason for that is because the Sea of Galilee is shaped like a violin.

Kinneret was my true birthplace. I probably spent as much time in the lake as I did out of it and that includes sleep, work and study time. I have wondered many a time what my life would have been like if I had been born in the mountains, forest or desert. Who knows? I do believe though that I was born there for a reason. A fish must be near water or it will die.

Kinneret is actually a lake, a lake that is fed by a few rivers and the most famous one is the Jordan River, which falls from the Lebanon mountains in the north. The Jordan River flows through the lake and exits in the south heading down all the way to the Dead Sea. It, in fact, acts as the physical border between Israel and Jordan.

Since I was a child, I was drawn to the water. I spent hours every day walking the coastline and staring at the water. My parents' house was literally 100 m from a small cliff, which cut into the lake. I had my little secret place there inside the bush on top of the cliff.

I used to lie there hanging over the cliff's edge marvelling at the water. The water reached the cliff edge and after a good rainy season, it rose to one meter up the cliff. This allowed me to watch the fish, especially the big black catfish and the many seasonal birds that came to feed. I felt comfortable near the water. It always soothed me and gave me a sense of open and unlimited space that extended into the horizon.

Many years later, my father championed a project to barricade the entire coastline with boulders. The seasonal western wind kept on bashing the cliff and eating into the land. I have no idea if it was really necessary, but the project went ahead and the sea was pushed away a few metres. The coastline has never been the same.

Before the project, I used to walk along that beach alone for hours. I would look for various flotsams and stare up at the cliff face. As a small child, I thought the cliff was as high as a mountain. Above the cliff, there were the fields of the neighbouring kibbutzim and many times little waterfalls were created from the irrigated water leaving the fields. That channelled its way to the sea and created little rivers and pods of water that attracted the fish. I used to track the fish and sometimes would catch a few. Most times, I would set some traps for the fish to go find later.

We all grew up fishing. There was nothing fancy about our fishing, just a simple rod, line and bait. We caught the fish and we brought them home to cook. We grew up with plenty of food and did not need to go hunting for fish. But it was a way of interacting with the water and my mum used to cook them very well. We never fished for fun though. Whatever we caught, we brought home, gutted it, cleaned it and cooked it. We did the same with pine mushrooms and sometimes wild geese. It was a good life, growing up in a kibbutz, which was pretty much like a farm with plenty of open space around us.

Later on in life, I developed a real distaste for hunting and any sport fishing. I have never really understood the kick people got out of catching an animal for fun and in a best-case scenario releasing it back. I also developed a strong sense of nature and its purity. I have tried hard to teach my kids not to pick up anything when we are in nature. Not even a small flower because it belongs there.

Our whole family was very connected to the sea. My mum used to swim almost every day, slowly and steady. My brothers and I used to drag our dad at sunrise to go fishing in remote places around the lake. Growing up by the lake we were either swimming or in the water somehow. The Jordan Valley, where I grew up, is around 200 m below sea level and it gets very hot during the summer. The water temperatures can rise to 30°C in the summer and possibly down to 16°C in the winter. Nowadays, I can't conceive of swimming at 30°C as I find it way too warm. I never liked the intense heat of the valley and the sea always provided me with shelter. I sometimes used to spend hours in the water, usually after school or work.

I took on sailing in the 420 Olympic dinghies following my brothers. The kibbutz had a couple of boats and lucky for me, no one hardly used them. So, when I reached 15 years of age and was allowed to take one of the boats, I literally spent eight days a week sailing in the lake. The valley had its regular afternoon thermal wind that came from the west, the Mediterranean sea. It used to come almost every day at around 3 pm. I would wait for it and when it arrived, the sea would go from a glass-like lake to a rough and angry woman. I loved it! I felt alive as I would crisscross that lake for hours, sometimes with friends but mostly alone. Sailing with me wasn't for the faint-hearted; I was a real adrenalin nut!

The boat had two sails, a main and a jib and a huge spinnaker. I had no problems on my own with two sails but with a rudder bit for the spinnaker, I needed another pair of hands. I felt so comfortable in the water that capsizing or dealing with a broken rudder or a dagger or any other accident for that matter didn't faze me at all. It was part of sailing in the strong wind and these things happened from time to time.

It was where I learnt the lesson of preparing for an adventure. It taught me to check everything on the boat that could have possibly caused me problems later on. I would check the sails for small tears or holes. I would check the cables and then all the moving parts of the boat. I would check for leaks and make sure I had a few extra items in case of an emergency. I also knew that if anything broke, it would be my responsibility to fix it. I had no problem with responsibility as long as I knew it was mine, and then I dealt with it.

When I was in the army, I used to take the boat out every time I got a weekend off and spend hours in the water. Although, while in the army, my home leave used to only be around a 24-hour stint. This equated to a good shower, handing over my dirty washing to my mum, a good meal and a warm bed for around 16 hours, and then back to the army. After the army, I was caught by the windsurfing bug. The first time I saw someone gliding over the water attached to a few poles and a board, I simply fell in love. It took over my passion for sailing.

I do remember a time when I was sailing in Kinneret, on my own, having a blast. The wind had picked up to above 30 knots and I, with my 59 kg of weight, wasn't enough to balance the boat. Every jibe was a suicide attempt, but I knew I had to get back home. I capsized several times but managed to get the boat back on track. I can't remember getting tired, but I always knew I couldn't desert the boat no matter what happened. I would stay with it until we both went down. Mainly because I knew I would be crucified if I lost the boat and secondly, I knew it was my safety float.

I must have capsized for the sixth time and as I jumped back on the dagger and turned the board around, I slipped. The mounting of the dagger had a loose screw sticking out and it just tore through the skin of my stomach leaving a deep long and nasty trail. I screamed and expressed my views to Poseidon but that was over quickly. I had to get back home.

Every time I got back from a sailing adventure, I would do a thorough body check. I used to find bruises and cuts, sometimes quite deep, and most times, I couldn't recall when I had received them. I felt like it was just the water protecting me as long I was with it. Many times, after many hours in the water, we used to spend the evenings comparing scars and treating them.

In the meantime, the cut on my stomach was not healing as per usual. Maybe because the blood was flowing or I saw it and it registered in my mind. And then the rudder just snapped and the boat went into a spin. I let go of the ropes as the sails were smashing around frantically like they were possessed by demons. I grabbed the slack in the ropes and jumped off the back of the boat. Placing the ropes between my teeth, I held on to the back of the boat with my hands. I was being dragged by the boat as I lay in the water behind it, but I managed to pull the main and get some tension in the sail. I used my body as a rudder while being dragged behind. All pain and panic disappeared and it was replaced by a huge sense of fun. It wasn't the first time I had tried this and it was the first time I was alone on the boat with a broken rudder. I was young and very fit (now I am just young) and I managed to navigate the boat, tacking widely to the shore. At one point my swimming trunks started slipping down towards my ankles and I managed to pull them off and throw them into the boat. So, there I was being dragged at high speed, naked, behind a renegade boat. It was super fun!

There were times when I miscalculated the waves and was bashed around a few times, but it was still just sheer euphoria for me. In the end, I managed to get back home after quite a few hours in the water. I got home just before sunset and found out that the water temperature had been around 28°C and the air temperature about 30°C, perfect conditions for me. I hooked up the boat, packed everything away and headed in for supper. I was ravenous. There is nothing like hours in the water to work up an appetite. But I did go passed the nurse to see my big cut, which turned out to not be too serious. Another awesome day in the water had come to an end. Life couldn't be better.

A couple of months later, I was caught in a similar situation. Nothing broke that time, but the wind was gusting at around 40 knots and the boat capsized many times rendering me utterly exhausted. After many hours, I felt that I had nothing left in my arms. I lay on top of the capsized boat and let it drag me to shore.

Suddenly, a police boat arrived. I'm afraid I didn't have much respect for them as I had had a few encounters with them in the past and I wasn't even sure any of them could swim. They were all dressed in uniforms and it appeared that none of them had any intention of helping me. I told them to go away but they wouldn't. They said they had a duty to bring me back, but I refused to get on their boat. I wasn't going to just leave my sailing boat like that. I was threatened and shouted at but to no avail. Finally, I asked them to help me to unrig the boat and get everything on their big boat. I was nearly arrested or rather beaten for my stupid idea. They guys clearly had lost all sense of patience and humour. The policemen took out a long rope and decided to tie my boat to theirs and drag me to shore. I wouldn't let them do that either, which got them seriously upset. I was fine. I was in the water and in the water was safer than on their boat. If they dragged the boat upside down, it would have torn everything apart. It was madness, I needed to unrig it.

One of the policemen took out a huge knife and leaned down towards the rig trying to cut it all. I screamed at him to stop and begged for a few minutes to try and do it myself. I promised I would then go back with them. Diving down under the boat, I started to unrig it and managed to get it done, but the rig was too heavy and it was pulling down quickly. Luck must have been on my side that day because I felt the mast scarping the seabed. It was getting shallower at around five metres and I managed to balance the rig on the mast, in the water, upside down. Passing the rope to the policemen, they helped me lift the entire rig with the sales and the mast onto their boat. They were grumpy but happy to see it all sorted. I will have you know that at no point did any of them consider undressing and jumping in to help me. I noted the course of the waves and marked a landmark on the horizon where I thought the boat may wash up later once we had let it go.

Later on, around 8 pm, someone came to pick me up with the gear and took me home. As soon as I arrived, I changed, grabbed a torch and started walking the beach towards the place I thought I may find the boat shell. It was at 11 pm that I found it buried deep in the reeds. I still had to drag it back home in the water which was knee height, which took me another few hours. In the end, all was well. So, from a young age, I was always of the mind that one must never give up and never panic or at least try your best. It was a tough day and I deserved a real big meal.

Years later in 2006, I decided to come back and swim the length of the Sea. A couple of years before I swam the width, all alone. Omri, my mate, dropped me on one side of the lake by Tiberias, in a swimming costume and goggles. I just dived in and swam across, alone, with no boat and no feeding. I felt very comfortable in this lake called the sea. The water was warm and I drank it when I got thirsty. It was only a 10km swim and 3h later I walked out to my Kibbutz beach. No one knew where I appeared from. It was great fun,

Me with my fantastic four

The swim is across the length of the lake around 21km, subject to currents, water conditions and the direction of the swim. To compare, a swimmer can lose between 50m-100m in distance per kilometre in the sea (5%-10%). The Kinneret water temperature goes up to 30C and air temperature can exceed 40C in summer and the Kinneret lies more than 200m below sea level.

I contacted the Israeli Masters Swimming Association and asked for their assistance with the swim and the idea took off in an amazing way. I knew Gershon quite well, a seasoned top Israeli swimmer and a friend. By 2006 I completely lost contact with all my old friends in Israel. I left in 1987 and time just flies. It was amazing how swimming has connected me back to Israel and allowed me to meet many newfound friends.

Before I knew it, my solo crossing of the Sea of Galilee turned into an Israeli military operation. Gershon asked me if I mind if a couple of other local swimmers will join me as a memorial swim for Ron Arad. Arad was an Israeli pilot captured in Lebanon in 1986. His state and whereabouts are unknown – there was a $10m prize on the internet for anyone who provides information that may lead to his current position. The swimmers were air force pilots from his squad and the symbolic connection was 20 years since his capture and 20km across the lake.

The swim was organised like a military operation, Kayaks, boats, doctors, approvals, family, friends and communication were all prepared meticulously. Two of us were planning to swim the entire length of The Kinneret, Adi Pereg and myself. Adi was a friend and pilot with Ron Arad and also used to swim for Israel in his youth. We were accompanied by around 10 more swimmers who swam with us on and off. I had my whole family there. My four kids, Kaitlin, Jordan, Gilad and Neve. Neve's middle name is Kinneret the Hebrew name for the sea of galilee. My brothers came to the finish as well as my late mom.

We decided to start the swim at 5:30 am estimating around 7h in the water. The heat was a real concern given the risk of sunburn and dehydration. Wake up call at 3 am. After coffee and a peanut butter sandwich, we met at Tiberias harbour at 4:30 am. We sailed to the starting point, next to the place where the "miracle of the five loaves and two fish" apparently occurred.

The air is cool and the water is pleasant and the first 5km went quickly, the sun was gently rising over The Golan Heights. I breathe to the right side, so swimming from North to South, gave me the entire east side of the sea mountains as my view. On the other side, we had a view of the Golan Heights, Kibbutz Maagan (where I grew up) and the Jordan Valley. Overall, the swim took around 7 hours, as expected. We stopped every 30 mins for a feed (although the energy gel tasted so bad you really wished the swim to be at an end). I didn't enjoy the high-water temperature. After years of swimming in the Atlantic Ocean in Cape Town, 28C felt like a hot Jacuzzi. With my longest previous swim being 10km, the Kinneret swim brought a whole new dimension to long-distance swimming for me. Mentally, swimming for seven hours is quite lonely in all sensory aspects. One tends to cocoon oneself from the surroundings and try to find a place devoid of thoughts. The second lesson was about the impact on the body. My left shoulder gave up around the sixth hour and I found myself having to throw it forward every stroke, knowing that it could cause some damage. I knew that my training program was too light for the challenge, but I relied on my mental strength. I had the flu when I arrived in Israel so I was swimming with antibiotics (not advised but not my first time). The reception at the end was overwhelming. We had huge reception from kayaks, swimmers, and families. Since that swim was done many times and become a very popular open water long-distance swim in Israel. Dominated by the Israeli wonder woman Avishag.

I had a special swimming cap made with the Swim for Peace writing on each side. Unfortunately, two days after the swim a new war started on the Lebanon border following the kidnapping of a young Israeli soldier and a few shells fell in Tiberias not too far from our hotel. The swim obviously didn't achieve its objectives, I guess we need to keep on swimming.

Sea Of Galilee, Lake Kinneret, Swim for Peace and Ron Arad

Chapter 17
Antarctica I – Guinness World Record

On 4 February 2008, at 6:25 pm, the phone rang. It was Robyn from White Desert expeditions, the company organising the Antarctica trip, calling to say that we were ready to go. Great! Time to pour a glass of single malt whisky and get ready.

I arrived at Cape Town airport with a backpack and my Baffin boots, bearing a striking resemblance to *Happy Feet*. We checked in and on the flight information screen, in between Amsterdam and Paris, there was a place called Novo. Most people didn't realise that this would be our final destination in Antarctica. Our plane was a big Ilyushin Russian aircraft. We were accompanied by a bunch of scientists going to Antarctica for the winter shift, mostly Russians with a sprinkling of some Germans and Norwegians.

As we boarded, there was a big table with a projector on top and a portable screen. This was the in-flight entertainment system. The plane could carry 80 passengers to a maximum of 20 tons and the back of the plane was for cargo, the front for passengers. In Antarctica, every kilogram of cargo is worth a lot of money, so no spare weight capacity is unused. Every free seat would be disassembled and replaced by more cargo. Antarctica closes in mid-March for eight months when it is totally inaccessible. Even during summer, a cargo ship can wait for weeks at the sea barrier before it can offload its cargo.

I sat in 5A, a window seat. Wonderful! I really wanted to see the approach view of Antarctica. But there are no windows. I was sitting in by the wall, bare metal pipes next to me and the wall itself seemed to move around a bit. The ceiling was the internal organ of this aircraft and the oxygen masks looked as though they had come from World War One. Actually, the whole plane looked like a World War One 'mission improbable'. Trying to stretch your legs could have ended in serious injury due to the vast amount of sharp metal everywhere. The noise was deafening, so we were supplied with earplugs. Unfortunately, they were not a patch on Bose sound reduction earphones. I fell asleep and woke up as we descended into Novo, the Russian airbase. Apparently, everyone noticed that I was the only one who managed to sleep the entire flight. Well, I had learnt how to from my five years in the Israeli army. Sleep time was a priceless commodity, one shouldn't waste it.

Forty people changed in the plane into Antarctic clothing and all in the space of 10 square metres. It was comical, to say the least. It was 3:30 am in Novo with a ground temperature of -10°C, it was essential to ensure you dressed properly. Out of the plane, the view was so surreal, it was unbelievable. It was a vast space of endless white stretching forever. With the sun up, it was extremely bright. We packed our stuff into two snow vehicles and headed to our camp. The camp looked like an olden day's polar exploration camp, with some added comfort.

Moment of truth – first time to get into 0C water – I didn't know what will happen

The Test Swim – 5 February 2008

I managed to convince Paul, Patrick and my "documentary" team (Denise and Peter, who decided to come to my assistance with the camera and the video) to go for a test swim. We climbed straight out of our camp over the hill to a frozen lake created by the glacier nearby. The lake was mostly frozen with a very small open water patch at the other end. We got to the lake and realised that we would have to create a small swimming pool in order to be able to have enough space for a swim. I was starting to get tense inside having never been in such cold water and with little idea of what to expect. We started throwing small rocks to break the surface ice sheet, creating a 15 m channel in the frozen lake.

I was very nervous about the broken ice as it could have been very sharp, like big pieces of broken glass floating on the water. The ice was as thin as half an inch to an inch, very translucent. We created a nice channel and the time had come to test the icy waters.

Antarctica my first Ice Swim

The water temperature was somewhere just above freezing and just under 1°C. Paul put waders on and stood in the water up to his knees. Patrick was 'ready' to dive in in case of an emergency and 'my documentary team' were instructed to document everything regardless of any crisis or possible panic. The time had come. Clothes off, standing in my little black Speedo, a cap on (I wasn't using a cap for quite some time in my Clifton swims), goggles and I was ready. The aim was to try and do five minutes and see how I felt. I stood on the rock ready to get in, but I didn't want to dive as the lake was unsafe. So, I stepped forward and stopped. I focused and looked at the water having no idea what to expect. For all I knew, I could have jumped in and within a few seconds, it could have been the end of my Antarctic swim attempt. I couldn't get myself to jump in trying to delay the potentially embarrassing or stupid adventure. They say, 'The difference between stupidity and bravery is in the outcome.'

Cold water swimming made me think anew about myself. One thought was to focus on the issues at hand, like getting into cold water every Sunday over the past five years, regardless of temperature, water conditions as well as weather conditions. I established many little rules for myself, my little book of self-discipline. In one of Sir Ranulph Fiennes' books, he uses the quote, 'In an expedition, better learn to use self-discipline than having the humiliation of being disciplined by your teammates.'

One of my little rules was, 'You can linger for as long as you want, but when you start counting to three, there is no way back. You dive in at three regardless of anything.' One way to force your going is to start counting. So, I did that and jumped in. It felt wonderful, like jumping into a slush puppy without the straw. The cold wraps around you like a thick heavy blanket slows you down and focuses you. It wasn't nearly as bad as I expected. At some temperatures, it doesn't matter how cold it is, your skin goes numb in a second and you feel no pain, the pain came a few seconds later. And so, I started to swim.

Swimming felt great. It is one thing I feel very comfortable doing, swimming, head down, not letting the burning pain and headache distract me, just stroke, one, two, breath, one, two, breath, find the rhythm and suddenly, I am 100% fine. I actually enjoyed it. However, swimming up and down the channel proved more complicated than I had expected as I kept swimming into the ice bank, sometimes smashing it with my stroke and sometimes pushing it aside. Swimming the entire length of the Orange River teaches you many things and one of them is to adjust your stroke to the environment, rocks, bank, waves and the occasional boat trying to run you over (accidentally).

I was going back and forth, replying to Patrick and Paul's questions, "I am okay." In the last lap, I swam over the ice stopping with the ice sheet halting at my neck. I stopped, panicked immediately and reached to my neck, rubbing it with my frozen hand, looking at my fingers to see for signs of blood. I know from windsurfing for hours that once you are finished, you must dry yourself and then pay attention to the pains in your body to discover possible cuts. There was a time once when it required a rush to the hospital for serious stitching after a piece of the skin of my foot was missing. Gruesome as it sounds, one of my windsurfing mates came to my room later on that day with the missing piece of skin that was hooked to the side of my surfboard.

I have heard many stories about how dangerous the ice can be but luckily, there was no blood and no cuts, just a choke by the ice and a few missing heartbeats. I was feeling fine but my hands felt as if they had expanded significantly. I felt as if I had massive swimming paddles on my hands. My feet were fine though besides that I couldn't feel them, that was nothing to worry about.

Six and a half minutes were gone and it was time to get out of the water. I found it quite difficult to walk on the rocks with no sensation in my feet, but Patrick and Paul helped me out to the rocks. I was feeling good, completely in control of my body aside from my hands. They were very sore like I had dipped them in hot oil. Patrick advised me to shake my arms violently to try to resume normal circulation to my fingers. Finally, after about five minutes, my fingers started to feel normal again. Funny enough, when I got back to the tent and tried to access my laptop to download the pictures taken, the fingerprint recognition pad didn't like my finger, until I rubbed it aggressively a few times to warm it up.

We hiked back to the camp for about 35 minutes and I felt really alive. Step one and two in the attempt has been tested. Step one was a possible cardiac arrest from the shock of entry to freezing water and step two was hyperventilation and lack of ability to swim in the first few minutes. Now it was time to get ready for the attempt and sort out the logistics around that, which appeared to be more complicated than the swim itself.

Diving in for a quick swim with my red underwear that made me famous

Training for the Swim

At the time of my swim, ice swimming (which was yet to be coined a year later when I founded IISA) didn't exist. I had basically no one to ask about the risks, the procedures, the recovery. I was walking into completely unknown territory.

Training for the swim had three parts:

1. Research
2. Physical
3. Mental

Research

Months before the swim I started searching the Internet for people who had completed cold water swims. I watched endless videos of cold swims, news alerts and medical research. I was amazed by how relatively little information there was. Eventually, I managed to get hold of Lynne Cox, who was kind enough to listen to all my questions and she gave me very careful advice, tips and moral support.

I read quite a lot about hypothermia to try and understand what to expect, but there was very little understanding of hypothermia as a result of cold water swimming. Plenty of environment-related hypothermia or accident-related but not about cold water swimming.

I managed to find some very interesting video clips on YouTube that helped me to see various people plunging into ice water, their body language, facial reactions and recovery process. It helped me loads to understand the parameters of what I should try and do and where the possibilities and the limits were.

Physical

I followed fellow swimmer's preparations for various cold swims and read some. There were a few issues to consider:

1. Cold water swimming versus ice bath training.
2. What temperature do I need to experience and for how long before I plunged for a swim at -10°C.
3. Walk-in or dive in?
4. Head up with breath stroke for the first few minutes or head down and crawl immediately.
5. Time spent in cold water versus speed (knowing I only intended to swim 1 km in ice water).
6. Previous swimmers put on 20 kg in the months before the swim, did I need to?

I had to be determined about all the issues before the attempt. There would be no time to test these issues at the attempt time.

So, this is what I did:

1. I took Lynne's advice and decided on cold water swimming and no ice baths. It was a good decision.
2. I decided to focus on a minimum of 25 minutes to a maximum of 45 minutes in as cold conditions as possible. In hindsight, I should have spent a minimum of an hour every time.

3. I tested diving in and it worked great for me. It forced me to get used to the cold immediately and focus on the swim. Once you get used to it, the pain is reduced significantly (also the mental pain).
4. I decided to train without a swimming cap for the last few weeks. It helped tremendously. I forced myself to put my head down and swim until the severe ice cream headache was gone, but it did take a while initially. Highly recommended.
5. I reduced my mileage in the last six weeks prior to the swim. I would recommend keeping the usual mileage and keeping top fitness without losing weight if possible. The cold water slows you down immensely. If it is a short swim, 20–30 minutes, strength is very useful. I should have done more middle-distance fitness.
6. I decided to try and put on 20 kg, bearing in mind that I was the heaviest I had ever been at 75 kg. I struggled to put on weight in an evenly distributed fashion. So, 20 kg meant increasing my body weight by 26.66% while maintaining my 'Brad Pit' proportions. Needless to say, I did try hard, possibly not hard enough, and I managed to lose 1 kg (not gain) by the time had come. There was probably too much pressure so I gave up on that idea. I don't know how much would it have helped me anyway. I don't carry significant layers of fat and I am sure it would have helped if I had stayed much longer. But possibly not that significant for a 20–30 minutes swim.

I ended up swimming every day (at least once) in the eight to ten weeks prior to the swim in Clifton 4th. I swam in rain and howling winds as well as with beautiful sea and stunning views on the beach. I had great support from fellow swimmers who joined me on a regular basis and provided encouragement and references to some of the shrinks they know.

Water temperatures presented five days of an opportunity to swim at 8°C. That was super cold! On average, the water temperature was around 11–12°C. If I could have done some other swims at around 5°C, I think it would have helped but only if I have done so for some time. An accidental dip doesn't do much for acclimatising but rather puts your extremities under unfair stress.

Mental

The research and talking to others helped a lot. I created some expectations about what might happen and how to deal with it. I wasn't afraid of the pain. It was something that I dealt with until it went away and it usually goes away after a while in cold water. The commitment was the most important issue. I knew that logistically and physically, I would have plenty of reasons to abort the attempt, but like my Robben Island night swim, I knew I had to be 100% committed and make sure I managed the risk properly.

It worked. I spent hours, every day, looking at the environment and the lakes around on Google Earth. It was amazing going there in the middle of nowhere and recognising the lakes. I visualised a lot of my entry into the water, breathing, strokes, views and the surroundings. It helped tremendously to feel as if I had almost done it already. I couldn't, however, simulate the pain and the impact of the cold water on my skin, muscles and breathing. So, my strategy was 'whatever happens, don't panic!'

The Visit to the Indian Camp – Swim Logistics

The next day we spent most of the day trekking to an iceberg and around it. We learnt how to set a 'dead man' and three-point support for ice climbing. Deadman is an additional safety setup if all three points get lost. Ice climbing is a very serious task and safety is crucial. The ice is very slippery, hard and sharp. A mistake can be very painful.

We ended the day having a picnic at the top of the giant rock next to the camp, Nunatak in Eskimo or Shivalinga, Shiva's penis in Indian, overlooking the camp and the vast Antarctic space. We got back to the camp at 4 pm exhausted after seven hours of ice climbing. Patrick said we needed to move to the Indian camp as we had a meeting with the camp leader at 5 pm. A one-hour walk to the Indian camp turned out more like a one-hour 40-minute walk. We bumped into an Indian guy out for his daily evening walk and found out that he was the camp shrink. He is busy reading Patrick's book right now.

We met the camp leader, Jan-Paul who was extremely friendly and accommodating. It was a few degrees below zero and he had a fridge in his room. It seemed like swimming in the Indian lake was too complicated. He may have required permission from India and he was concerned that if things went wrong in the swim, it may cause some noise in India. We talked about swimming in a lake nearby and using their helicopter to drop a boat and a generator at the lake. We met the Indian doctor, Surgeon Lieutenant Udaya IB (I prefer to call him doctor not surgeon though), a great guy with loads of energy and a keenness to help. The decision was taken to swim in a lake nearby. The lake was called Long Lake and it was halfway between our camp and the Indian camp, about a one-hour trek in the mountains.

We agreed to meet midday and the doctor would come to our camp so we could go together to the lake. We decided to tie a 30 m rope to an empty weight belt around my hips and have someone walk on the side of the lake next to what I saw. The Indians were absolutely fantastic. Their kindness and support were great. Currently, they are in the process of trying to change the lake's name from Long Lake to Lake Ram through the Indian and the Antarctic authorities. (Ram is a Hindu god. Who knew my name would be so useful one day?)

Patrick managed to get Garry Kirstin (current Indian cricket team coach) to sign on a cricket shirt as a thank you note to Maitri (the Indian station). I just gave them all South African Protea caps (respect).

The Swim

The day arrived and I spent the morning preparing the logistics, which were mainly driven by Patrick and his team. Needless to say, I couldn't have done it without their support and keenness, including their moral support, interest in my swimming and enthusiasm. My support team consisted of Patrick, the expedition leader and the co-founder of White Desert, Paul, A seasoned polar explorer whose been everywhere with ice and Inge, a hardcore Norwegian explorer and a very talented guy, strong as an ox. They all got roped in very excited to see this mad man attempting to swim in 0C in Antarctica.

We decided to get to the Lake ourselves and let the other guys on the tour meet us there later. We were up, all getting there together, including the Dr Udaya. Inge carried a generator in his backpack and the doctor insisted that we have some power if he needed to use some of his power tools. We decided to set the course from the icy part of the lake along its left bank. We set a flag every 200 m with the tent at the first 200 m mark. The plan was to swim 200 m to the tent, continue for another 400 m, a total of 600 m) and get back to the tent which would make it 1 km. If I felt strong, I would have continued another 200 m and another and another…

All was set and we started the pre-swim brief. We decided that Inge would run next to me with the 30 m rope. Patrick would be walking in the water in a dry suit and Paul would follow with the doctor on the bank. The routine was to give me a yank on the rope every 200 m and for me to signal back a thumbs up. If I shook my hand, it meant no sense of humour. If I waved my hand, it meant 'please take me out now.'

Antarctica GWR Swim starts, rope attached for safety

Dr Udaya started briefing the team about CPR, cardiac arrest and hypothermia on premature termination of the swim. That was my cue to go and start focusing at the start. I wasn't going to listen to what they would do to me if I failed. Anyway, I wouldn't be much help and I trusted them to deal with it or me. I went to the start and changed into my Speedo, goggles and my cap. I didn't use any lubrication for chafing or greasing for insulation. I covered myself with my Antarctic down jacket and waited.

Soon the team arrived at the start and the doctor decided to take my heart rate and pulse. My heart rate was much higher than usual and my pulse was around 84 (my resting pulse is around 50). The doctor got really stressed and recommended that I sit down and relax. I was relaxed, but it was cold outside with nothing on and I assumed that my body was anticipating my anxiety about the swim, possibly in a positive way, preparing me.

Nevertheless, I sat down for a minute and decided that it was as calm as I could be, so time to swim. I took off the jacket, hooked the rope around me and I stepped into the water. The water was shallow so diving was too dangerous. I stepped in to hip deep and then dived in. I already knew what to expect, but it was different. My hands didn't hurt that much, but my breathing was very tight. I put my head down and stroked slowly and rhythmically to calm my breathing. My breathing was my main focus of the entire swim. I took in very cold air straight to the lungs and it felt very thin like my lungs were tight the whole way.

The swim itself went great. The first 200 m went fine although I kept hitting the rope with my left hand and almost decided to take the belt off, however, I knew I didn't want to put my team at that risk, so I kept on swimming. Inge adjusted the slack significantly, so I didn't touch the rope anymore, but instead, I had a 30 m rope dragging in the water behind me. The rope slowed me down considerably, however, the great benefit of ice water is that the cold focuses you so much that you hardly notice anything else.

Before the swim, Doctor Udaya put the fear of God in me and I don't get scared easily. He explained to us the increased risk of cardiac arrest after 15 minutes of swimming when the body's focus shifts from protecting its extremities to protecting its vital organs. He also mentioned that there was a very low chance of reviving a person from cardiac arrest due to hypothermia. It was a very good dose of sense that knocked into me at the right time. I knew I had to do 1 km but I also knew that if I stayed in the water for close to 30 minutes, who knew how my body would react.

I am convinced that you can train your body significantly to deal with prolonged swims in ice water, but I always remember the saying, 'The difference between bravery and stupidity is in the outcome', so I decided to hedge my chances and focus on 1 km.

At the 600 m mark, I turned around and knew I was going to do a 1 km and I also wanted to finish then. I made a mistake and accelerated my stroke rate with only 400 m to the end. It was a bad mistake as my breathing got out of sync and I started to worry. I focused on the sight of the tent and swam towards it. I could feel that my stroke was losing its finesse and I started to struggle.

When I got to the 50 m mark, my mental state collapsed. But I only needed a few more strokes and then I made it to the end, too cold to smile and simply focused on the recovery. The real risk started then when the core body temperature continues to drop rapidly and you stop generating heat. I usually compare it to the stories I have heard about the descent from Mount Everest. The most fatal mistakes are done at that stage.

I was helped into the tent. I dried myself and covered my body with the down jacket, getting into a laying position. Apparently, the tent was boiling hot, but I was very cold. My skin was burning and every time someone touched me, I would jump. My skin temperature was close to 2–3°C and the normal temperature should be around 37–38°C). I felt waves of nausea and I couldn't drink the hot chocolate or sugar water the doctor was offering. I must admit, I had no idea what to expect and that added significantly to my anxiety. I saw Paul taking his shirt off and on asking why he replied that the tent was too hot. I realised it was to aid more rapid recovery and it did help. I was fully recovered within 15–20 minutes. It was the first-ever recovery from an Ice Swim. I had no idea what to expect and everyone around me knew significantly less than me. The price of pioneering.

I dressed, went outside and we all hugged each other, taking some pictures. The doctor told me that the odds he had given a successful swim were quite low. I should have put some money there. It was all very surreal and still today the actual swim seems unreal and remote. I think I focussed so hard on my mental state before the swim that when it was done my brain went to Mauritius for three weeks of recovery.

After recovery euphoria at "lake Ram" Antarctica GWR

We got our stuff and hiked back to camp, which took an hour. It was done. I loved it and I would do it again and again if I could.

I don't consider myself superior in any aspect, definitely not physically. The swim proved to me that many of the Cape Town cold water swimmers I know could have done the swim, having prepared themselves properly. Preparation is critical and understanding your body's reaction and function under these conditions is also crucial. The rest…is all in your mind. I already decided there and then that I want to spread the word on ice swimming. But I never expected to look back in 13 years and see swimmers from 40 countries around the world competing in a one km swim at 0C.

Chapter 18
Lake Zurich Swim

Swimming Lake Zurich mid-winter – the swim that created IISA

It was time to test the limits of the ICE. I came back from Antarctica, and I knew I had much more in me. I had to find the limits.

Well, there we are again, pushing the envelope another few inches. I travelled to Geneva in December 2008. The lake was a cold 5°C and there was some ice around the fountain. I had an irresistible urge to jump in and swim (luckily, I didn't). Since then I had accumulated significant experience in cold water swimming and it was time to fulfil the urge to swim in a snowy European lake.

There are plenty of frozen lakes in Europe and through time, we may swim a few of them, but Lake Zurich seemed like a good start. The Europeans are known for their winter dips in frozen lakes and icy water, however, long-distance swimming in these waters is not common or done at all. Therefore, it was going to be an interesting challenge.

Last February, I swam 1 km in Antarctica at just under 1°C water temperature. Aside from the swim, which was also an interesting challenge, the logistics were the real issue. We hoped that this time it would be safer because we were planning a slightly longer swim.

We contacted Amanda Picard (ex 'Missy' Grendon) a South African living in Zurich, a top ex-South African swimmer. Amanda was the one to suggest that we swim in Lake Zurich so she could enlist the Zurich swimming club to help us. That sounded great, so we set the date for the end of January 2009, which happened to be the coldest time of the year. Amanda was organising a boat, a doctor and a few friends to assist us with the swim safety.

Winter temperatures in Europe can vary, however, so far 2009 was their coldest winter in 12 years. The current temperatures in Zurich were recording lows of -11°C and highs of -5°C. Lake Zurich seldom freezes over, maybe once every 15 years, so we hoped the winter was not going to cover the lake with ice. The business of breaking 3 km of ice for a swim seemed like a complicated task.

I asked Andrew to join me. He has also become a veteran cold-water swimmer. It was time to test him on the ice. He should not have any problems with it though. Andrew and I left on the 27 January 2009 to Zurich for the attempt.

We were not sure about the course and distance as it would be subject to water temperature and safety. Lake Zurich is a freshwater lake, so it freezes over at 0°C unless the water flow is too fast for it to freeze.

We assumed a slow swimming speed of 20 min/km, although we usually swim quite a bit faster, however, the cold water slows you down significantly and if we wanted to cover some distance, we had to make sure our breathing was under control all the time. The cold water tightens your muscles dramatically and the only way to be able to move and cover the distance without panic is to control your breathing while inhaling air, which was a few degrees colder than the water!

The plan so far was as follows:

If the water temperature was between 1–2°C, we would attempt a mile swim in three minutes.

If the water temperature was between 2–3°C, we would attempt a 2 km swim in 40 minutes.

If the water temperature was above 4°C, we would attempt a 3 km swim in one hour.

We were not sure which one would be more challenging, but at those temperatures, every degree would make a big difference and time spent in the water was critical. It would be difficult to comprehend that at 2°C, which is extremely cold, moving to 1°C would be twice as cold. We were swimming at 9°C the other day, which was clenching to most parts of the body, so you can imagine swimming in three or nine times colder water (1–3°C) would be excruciating. It would be like going to Zurich with the South African rand. It was only about five times more expensive, so no real comparison. We would deal with each swim as they came.

Logistics

- We would have a small boat with a doctor and an experienced swimmer on board. Although we intended to swim close to the bank, it would be very cold and we couldn't assume that people on the lakeside would just dive into the icy water if we required help.
- We would have a vehicle nearby to transport us to a warmer place if required.
- Amanda and possibly others would accompany us along the lakeside on foot or bicycle weather dependent.

The conditions could vary significantly. It could be clear of snow and the sun could be out, but it could also be still and very fresh with super cold water. So far, it was the coldest winter Europe had had for many years, so it seemed like it would be chilly in Zurich till the end of January.

We started training a week ago swimming in the Atlantic Ocean. We tried to swim around 3 km a day with a longer swim on the weekends. We were swimming 30 minutes to an hour in cold water and for an hour in the pool for aerobic fitness. We too had been swimming without a swimming cap for some time.

The coldest we had so far, without a cap, was 45 minutes at 9°C. It takes around five minutes to get rid of the immense ice cream headache. It feels like someone has put your head in a big, tight vice and the pain wraps around your entire skull, which is quite unbearable. We needed to stop every 20 seconds to shake our heads in order to try and get rid of the vice. After around five minutes, the head goes numb and the pain goes away as well, but you still lose heat faster than normal. One is believed to lose 80% of one's body heat through the head, hence our training without a cap. Later on, I found it to be another icy myth. We intended to 'climax' our training in a Robben Island swim, without a swimming cap, on Andrew's 40th birthday at around 11C, which was on 21 of January. If we survived that, we thought we would be ready for a 3 km swim in a semi-frozen lake.

We planned to sort out safety and logistics on the 28 on arrival and do a test swim of at least 20 minutes on the 29. The actual attempt would take place on 30 January. We were as flexible as our safety team, so we didn't have much time to fool around.

The real challenge in this attempt was the time spent and the distance covered in these temperatures. The first 30 minutes should be bearable, assuming a water temperature of around 4°C. After that, swimming may become quite challenging with a loss of control of hands and fingers. Arms and shoulder muscles may also struggle to connect properly. This may slow us down quite a lot. If we manage that, the risk of hypothermia increases rapidly after around 40–50 minutes. Most research deals with cases of people falling into icy waters and the length of time they have managed to survive there. According to the literature available, surviving an hour in that water should be rather impossible.

I still believed that there was very little known about swimming in ice water and the recovery after the swim. Although we were not in the medical profession, I had accumulated a significant amount of experience in the past eight years, swimming all year round the world in cold water.

This was what we had accumulated collectively:

- I avoided hot showers immediately after the swim as it caused the blood to rush to my extremities and brought on serious nausea and possible fainting. It was not a good idea to lose control in a serious condition.

- I dried my body off as quickly as possible and got into dry clothing as soon as I exited the water. There was no time for dignity as the moisture acts like a fridge on your body.
- I would walk and move to continue generating heat. Avoid lying down, crumbling like a porcupine and shivering as it only works for a short time, and you lose control of the recovery process.
- A hot drink helped a lot to warm your frozen internal organs, but it shouldn't be too sweet or too hot. Your stomach muscles are still very tight and any extreme temperatures hitting them can cause issues.
- I would try to not shiver, if possible, but push the cold away mentally. This is probably the hardest part, but if you manage that, you recover faster. The shivering can get into an uncontrollable shaking of the body. It does generate heat, but also uses a lot of energy and can cause muscle spasms as well as the inability to take in hot fluids. I do it by trying to control my breathing after an icy swim.
- If the sun is shining, exposing the skin to vitamin D does a much better job than layers of clothing. Direct hot sun defrosts your skin and warms the blood close to the skin surface.
- Lying on hot surfaces like tar, rocks or cars in the sun warms you up very quickly too. Again, crumbling into a ball restricts the blood flow. Hot air is also very good, so climbing into a car and putting the heater on at full blast works a real charm.
- I believe that like in any other extreme situation, losing control of your body's actions is risky. Many times, like in Antarctica, you are not close enough to hospitals and proper medical care, so being able to manage the recovery process with the elements around you can save your life. It is critical to maintaining a cool (not cold) mind. Don't panic! Panic causes your body to do the wrong things. Focus! By doing so, the recovery will be much faster.
- As we mentioned, I may contradict some of the medical research undertaken, however, I have found through experience what works for me.
- A large part of the swim is psychological. It may sound strange, but if you want to feel the cold, you will and if you push it away, it works. Unfortunately, your body does present some limitations sometimes.

We swam every day in Clifton and we just knew that Zurich would be a great adventure.

At the time of writing this, the temperatures in Zurich were around -10°C at night and -5°C during the day. A tad nippy! Water temperatures in Camps Bay/Clifton had been around 20°C. We were getting very concerned about our cold water adaptation. In desperation, Andrew managed to organise an ice tub at the I&J fish factory in Woodstock. So, we started some ice tub training while praying for the southeaster to come and pound Cape Town enough to create an upswell. The southeast wind pushes the surface water out to sea, which brings the deeper water to the surface. This water comes from the cold current that makes our Atlantic seafront so cold. That was what we wanted and needed.

We had two tubs, we spent a total of ten minutes in the tubs of icy water and we were fine. My hands and fingers were extremely painful, but nothing fell off (lol!).

With 12 days to go, we were all set for our Zurich trip. The lake temperature was around 4°C during the day and 2°C at night. The outside temperature was around -5°C during the day and -10°C during the night. So, it looked like it was going to be a day event.

We arrived in Zurich, grey, cold and very expensive. We met the team and went through a thorough medical check by Professor Beat Knechtle, a mad sports scientist and athlete who just came back from 10 ironmen in 10 days. Amanda organised a lot of media attention for us which wasn't our focus, but we played the game. I knew I am going to focus on a world record swim and I needed a clear peaceful mind.

We decided to explore the course. The idea was to finish just after the bridge where the lake turns into a small river. It was close to the road and a car would take us to a nearby recovery facility as we finish. We started walking in the opposite direction measuring 3km. 3km never looked so long before. We walked and walked in the icy cold air thinking "we have to swim this, practically naked with a cap and a pair of goggles." Andrew was panicking. We walked back and, on the way back, we decided to cut it short. We identified a good place to enter the water by the casino, which was around 2.3km from the finish. It was an amazing mental thing for me. After trying to get a 3km swim into my head the drop to 2.3km made it feel like an easy task. The power of our mind.

We went for a wee test swim. the water was 4C and the air was significantly colder. Andrew in his typical fashion slipped on the slippery slope and made it faster to the water. We had a good test swim. People stopped to look at us as madmen. What's new? We had an evening briefing, and the swim was on. Andrew was panicking. He started sending messages to his wife and kids as if he may not be coming back. It wasn't good for me. I never think like that. Regardless of great whites, icy waters, and big waves I always believe I will be coming back. It's a mindset, maybe stupid or brave, who knows. I don't like to do anything believing the odds are against me. I decided decades ago, that I am not a gambler. It doesn't mean that things can't go wrong, but I like to assess, study and calculate. Once I believe the odds are significantly in my favour, I have no problem going ahead. Success is never guaranteed. I am always aware of it. But, that's an integral part of the challenge. I remember telling Andrew it will be fine and we will not push ourselves to a place of no return. It's a challenge, not a war.

We met early morning for some more medical checks. We were fine albite slightly high blood pressure. Later on in Ice Swimming, I realised that most of us

Lake Zurich Ice Swim – the first Ice Mile IISA ID #1

blood pressure rises before a swim, it's conditioning and anxiety. What is amazing is how quickly our blood pressure settles down once we start swimming. We had four water police boats with a TV crew and supporters. It was a big and new thing in Zurich. They sometimes cross the river on new year's eve, which is around a 100m swim. But we were going to swim 2.3km.

We were ready, walking into the water. I dived in and started to swim. Andrew, surprised, had no choice but to follow my dive and chase me. The lake was cold, 4C and the air was chilly with a wind chill factor of -7.5C°. The sky was grey and so was the air. We had boats on both sides and beautiful swans leading the way. It was another surreal swim. We swam at the same pace next to each other. Andrew set his mind on a tree that marked the 1km. It was his first ice swim and he wanted to do at least 1km. I wanted to finish. After the 1km mark, Andrew started to slow down and I felt strong and started to push. Suddenly I saw Andrew stop. It was around 1.2km and Andrew just stopped and went vertical. I stopped as well (not recommended) and ask him what was going on. He decided he had enough, he was very cold and he achieved his 1km goal. I could stick around for too long or my swim was over. I saw then dragging him into one of the boats like a big seal. He lay down and they just covered him with blankets. I had to put my head down and continue swimming. I still had over 1km to go. I continued swimming. I was worried, but the ice focused on survival. At around 2km I was flat, my breathing was very intense and my arms so frozen I didn't feel like I am moving. I heard Amanda screaming support and waving a big South African flag. It gave me a little push. I had an agreement with Professor Beat that as long as he is happy, I will continue swimming. His wife was next to him taking my stroke rate every minute. I locked my eyes on him as he was waving his hand to carry on swimming. I saw the bridge approaching yet it looked miles away. I finally go to the bridge and I knew I have around 50m to the finish steps. However, the bridge was side and cast a wide shadow on the water under. It was as if I am approaching a dark tunnel while my mind was already seeing a dark tunnel and I was feeling as if someone is dimming the lights on my life. It was a scary place so as we went under the bridge I stopped and looked around to try and gain sanity. I didn't realise that a diver just jumped in behind me waiting to fish me out if I start sinking. I did a few breast strokes looking at the dim light at the end of this tunnel. It looked miles away. I also lost all the support. The boats couldn't go under, and it was just me alone with 50m to go after close to

2.3km in this dark tunnel infinite. I wasn't aware of the diver. The water under the bridge was dark and very deep, I knew I had to get out of there. I put my head down and stroked. Once I saw the light on the other side approaching me, I started to "smile" or whatever my frozen face could express. I saw the stairs and everyone screaming for support on the other side. I knew I had done it. I managed to get to the stairs, but I couldn't walk. I actually needed some help, and for those who know me well, I don't like help. I like to walk out by myself with dignity. Needless to say, I had no dignity left. I was limping into the back of a car covered with a big blanket. I managed to stutter "where is Andrew" I was worried. I was assured that he is recovering and is in good condition. That calmed me down and I started focusing on my recovery. I was in a bad shape, and I knew I am heading towards an unpleasant hard recovery. It was hard and again, I learnt a lot about that side of Ice Swimming. 30 minutes later I was back euphoric and in good shape. It was a world record but Ice Swimming wasn't recognised by anyone at that stage. It paved the way for many new records years later. Now Ice Swimming is a recognised sport and the Guinness World Record for distance swimming belongs to a young 32-year-old Polish polar bear name Krzysztof Kubiak. He swam 3.75km in 4.8C water and wind chill and 8C. Rather warm. I have no doubt the 5km mark will be achieved one day. But it will require speed and stamina yet to be discovered. Keep safe!

Chapter 19
The Scariest Ice Swim of Them All – Tyumen Siberia

Swimming in Tyumen, Lake of Champions outside temperature -33ºC, water at 0ºC

I have been travelling the world for ice swimming adventures and managed to meet many people and create many amazing friendships with people and remote places. The Russians have been working on the Bering Strait Swim for a few years; it is a huge project that has taken off later on, and I got involved in it as part of the organising team with Andrew. This led to a surprise invite to the Russian Winter Swimming Championship in Tyumen, the heart of Siberia, in mid-Siberian winter in extremely cold temperatures. The Russian somehow heard about some of my swims in Antarctica and my Discovery Channel "superhuman" show.

I knew I had to go. It sounded so mad, so remote. All I knew about Siberia was from horror stories of Stalin's days when political prisoners were to the Gulag, a hard labour prisoner camp and mining camps in the hostile Siberian winter.

I called my swimming mates at the time Kieron and Ryan and after long motivational speeches at my office, next to the world map, I managed to convince them to join me on this mad exciting adventure promising them fame, glory and a crazy swim.

Russia has been one of the leaders in winter swimming. The vast country with plenty of frozen territories has thought these tough people to adapt and adapt they did. No limits to the harshness of the Siberian weather would stop them from a swim.

Antarctica 2014, I took my swim mates to discover my beloved frozen continent

My Ice Face

This was Russia's first winter championship with people from all the remote corners of Russia and a few from around the world. We from Cape Town, South Africa won the record for the furthest distance travelled to participate in this wonderfully insane adventure. Placed in Tyumen, in a frozen lake just outside the big city. Surrounded by frozen forests, the organizers cut two 25m pools in the ice with two lanes each. Wooden decks as a start platform with wooden planks at around 1m deep all around the pool. You don't want anyone to disappear under the ice sheet into the lake. You will only find them in the summer (well preserved).

The competition had two days that split between 25m and 50m sprints on the first day and endurance swims on the second day. The facilities were sufficient but far from comfort and luxury. Our team of Kieron, Ram, Ryan and

I, all experienced extreme cold water and long-distance swimmers. We focused on the endurance event.

We arrived at Tyumen at night in flip-flops and a warm jacket. It was -26C outside and very windy. It took us a few minutes to find the car waiting to pick us up. The cold penetrated our clothing and lack of shoes and by the time we got to the car, we were desperate. We were so unprepared, in a typical South African macho, it nearly killed us on arrival.

In Prague before an Ice Mile – flip flops

We drove to our hotel in a snowstorm through a white forest, petrified. How on earth are we expected to swim in this weather. We knew we came here to swim a distance. At least 1km or more. I wasn't prepared to travel for less than a 1000m swim. Regardless of conditions. Arriving at the pool, an outdoor frozen hole in the ice sent cold panic down our spines. This winter was is about

10 to 15 degrees Celsius colder than usual. That means that the outside air temp was sitting around -25C on the first day. We come from Cape Town, a beach holiday town where a T-shirt and a pair of slops usually do the job. It is just impossible to explain how bitterly cold it is standing at -24C with light wind and snow and grey cloud cover. Between the jokes and chirps, we looked at each other and said, "ok, we need an exit strategy here, this is too insane". We looked around the facilities and got even more nervous. How are we expected to get after a frozen swim to a wooden sauna 200m away from the pool at -24C°? The swimming started, with loud announcements and cheers, all in Russian and we understood NOTHING. They kept on saying "Ram Barkai You Are". It took me a long time to realise that South Africa is pronounced UR (Or You are). We had to go for a medical check, still chirping, and maintaining a strong sense of humour to hide the chill down our spines. The warm room temperature was close to 0C° and it was tiny with everyone on top of each other. We found a corner to settle down. We were called to do the 50m swim. The swim itself was a breeze. You dive in (before diving was not allowed) in -25C into 0C water wearing a speedo, cap and goggles. It was simply insane, but it went very quickly and off to the Sauna.

The first day was over; we felt better and started to psych ourselves for the next day, suppressing an extremely strong urge to drink ourselves silly. The cold and the swim gives one such rush and sense of health and vigour, hard to explain unless you have done it. We managed to control our urge and only have a few whiskeys in a nearby sushi bar we found. Tomorrow we need to be ready at 8 am to leave for the pool. Sun only rises here at 10:30 am. INSANE!

We got to the pool at around 9 am, with no breakfast and a lukewarm cup of coffee. The day was significantly colder at around -30C°. Pool frozen solid, we found a frozen towel standing by the pool left from the day before. At this cold, there is no humidity, and the snow is just like sand, you are not able to make a snowball, it is just white powder. The intensity of the cold freaked us, we checked again all the safety facilities and procedures. Not an easy task when all is in Russian and our translator was also one of the main organisers. We had our own safety procedures and rules, and we like to be comforted by them. It was quite arrogant of us to think that we in Cape Town understand cold better than the Russians. We couldn't spend more than 10 minutes outside without having to rush back in and sit by the heaters and defrost our legs and faces. My video camera wouldn't work it was so cold. How are we going to spend 20 minutes in the water and swim? It just looked like an impossible challenge. We set down and had a wee powwow, people around us started to shorten the distance from a possible 800m or 500m to 150m or max 300m. Most of them are well-known hard-core cold-water swimmers. English Channel swimmers and other fits looked very pale at the thought of the endurance swim. We shared our fears with friends on Facebook and we got the typical responses of South African males "stop complaining, man up and do it…" thank you for these encouraging words. The South African females were gentler with "you can do it, but please be careful".

The time has come for the medical check, one of the extreme swimmers was disqualified by the doctor with very high blood pressure. This didn't help our anxiety and heart rate. Kieron went in first and he came out with "I am fine, what's now? exit strategy one has gone". I went in second and came out with flying colours. "Right, Ryan is our only hope" Ryan went in and stayed, and stayed… Finally, I went in to check on Ryan. "The doc is not happy" Ryan said, "Blood pressure is very high". Ryan had a heart condition we all knew about. The doctor told Ryan to come back in half an hour for another check. Sense of humour and chirps died. We found a warm corner and had a debate, what do we do now? I said to Kieron that we are a team. I convinced them to come and therefore as a team we swim the same distances and look after each other. Kieron agreed with me. Ryan wasn't sure about the strategy. His approach was, that we all swim what we want.

The decision was mixed with some possible relief but a strong sense of "we came here to swim!". Suddenly from desperately trying to get out the swim, I had a strong desire to swim, to face the challenge and show ourselves that we can! The next half an hour was very tense. Rumours started flying that the hardcore SA team is bailing out. We knew that there are very high expectations here. Most knew of me and my Antarctica swim and the Discovery Channel program "Superhuman showdown" and now we are letting them all down. We withdraw to our corner, warming our frozen limbs and waiting. Next thing Ryan was called to see the Doc again. After a lengthy wait, Ryan comes out thumbs up. I am not sure if it was the right decision, but the Doctor said it's ok.

Great, our mind was getting into the right place now. "We are swimming and we are going to do it!" Focus and focus…here we come.

The Russian swam first and it was getting colder and colder, it was around 4:00 pm that I heard my name assuming it was swimming time. The temp outside was -33C. I changed into my swimming gear, a jacket and flip-flops and off I went out to -33C to swim in 0C water.

I got to the pool took my jacket off ready to start, in Speedo briefs, cap and goggles to get called in again "you swim later, go wait inside" What a mind @#$%. I went inside to defrost and wait. Very little conversation, we were very worried about the recovery process, we didn't know how or what and basically we had to let go and trust the Russian to look after us. That in itself didn't do good for our minds. Finally, at 4:30 pm I was called to swim. We all decided to do 1km and that's it. No bravery or heroes, we need to come home alive! Everything outside was sticky. At -33C everything is frozen in seconds. A female swimmer just finished her short swim, head up breaststroke and no goggles. Her eyelashes froze and she couldn't open them. They basically dragged her to the sauna to slowly defrost her eyes. Moist in the nose froze solid; breathing was like inhaling wasabi, slow shallow intakes. Any facial hair or long hair exposed to the icy air just froze. The water looked surprisingly inviting at Zero degrees Celsius.

Arriving for an Ice Swim, serious and focused

It was utter madness. Still, today when I get asked "what was the hardest or scariest swim ever" this swim comes to mind. I got to the pool, took my clothes off checked my goggles and got ready. Soon the call to start came and I just dived in and started swimming, my hands and feet froze so quickly that it almost numbs the pain. Every stroke a wet arm gets out of the water at -33°C for a few seconds. Water conducts heat 30 times faster than air. Every stroke, as your arm is out of the water the ice formed a thin layer around my skin to melt in the warm 0C° as it entered the water. Breathing was surprisingly fine. I was aware of breathing all the time. The air felt thick in my lungs but I felt as if I did get my oxygen and by the time it hit my lings it was warmish.

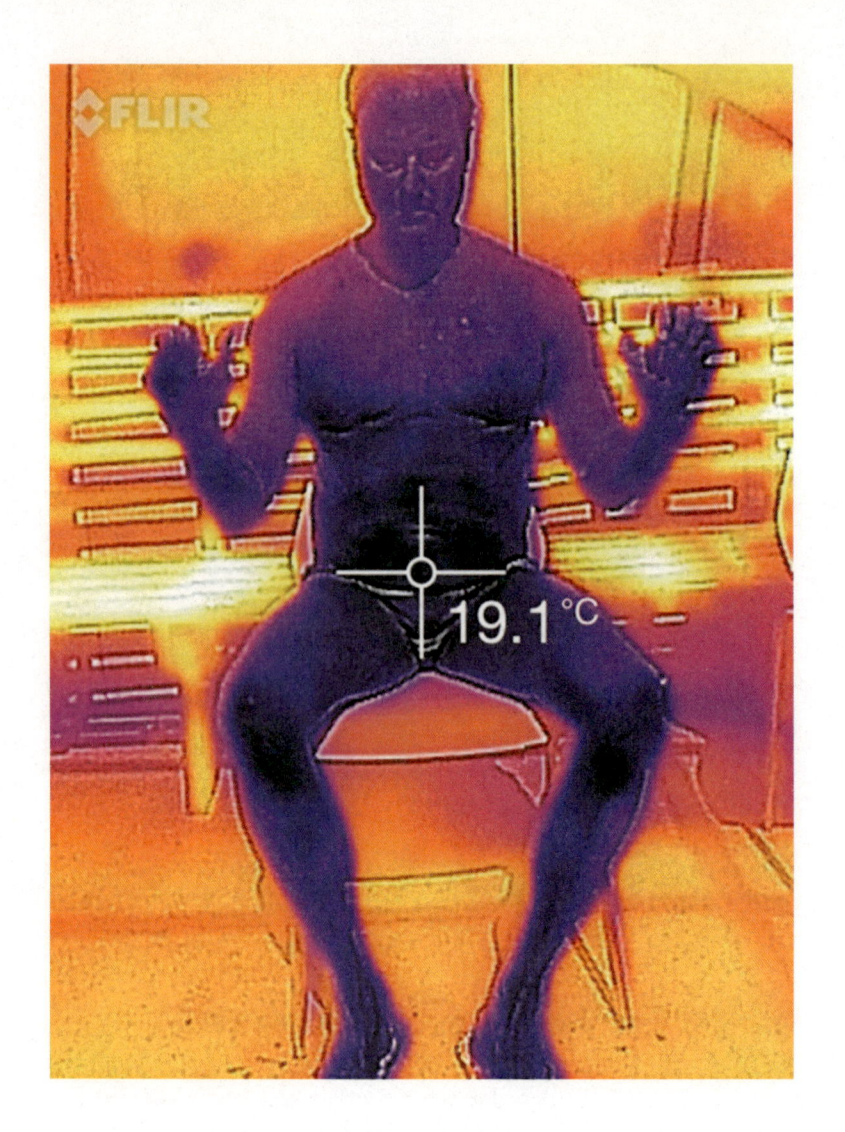

Sauna after the swim

Turning proved to be complicated by the fact that the wooden deck was frozen and a wet hand touching it can literally get super glued to the deck. You can easily leave some layers of skin on the deck without noticing. So touching the sides must be done underwater, pushing with the legs, not too hard so the breathing doesn't get jolted. One lap, two laps, and suddenly it was 40 laps. My mind was focused like a laser beam, excluding any sight, sound or thought that is not 100% related to the task of stroking through the water. When I finished, I couldn't touch anything, it was too dangerous, so I just raised my arms and waited to be dragged out. My skin was bright red almost glowing. By the time I got to the Sauna my skin is covered with a thin layer of ice giving the term icing the cake a new meaning. The real dangerous part, the recovery, was yet to start. When I was out, I realised I didn't feel the cold at all. Can an Ice Block feel the cold? It was -33C° outside, windy, and the sun was setting, I was wet, and I wasn't cold. I knew I had to get to the Sauna ASAP. The recovery was surreal. My mouth was foaming with blood and needless to say everyone was very concerned. Nuala and Irina were there, chatting rapidly in what sounded like Russian. I was coherent enough to ask myself "when did Nula learn Russian?". When you are that cold, everything moves much faster, as if you are in a slow-motion capsule and the world around you is speeding fast forward. Your core is extremely cold and so is your brain. The oxygen supply to the brain is compromised and you struggle to understand what is going on. Yet, I was focused and aware of everything. I realised that my tongue froze during the swim and as you swim to one side, my right, my tongue just dropped to the side of my mouth and as I breathing, I bit it quite hard. I was only noticed when I got out and started talking… It happened to me again later and the experience helped to calm down the panic around me. Recovery was as per usual, hard and intense. The little sauna was full of a few large Russian women led by Vici, Aleksander Brylin's wife. Later on, she saved me in recovery several times. She even came with us to Antarctica in 2018 and was in charge of recovery. It was a recovery method which, apparently, she developed, using towels soaked in hot water wrapped around you. I grew to love this recovery method and it works very well for me. The recovery process took me around twenty minutes. Hot and cold using water and wet towels to bring me back. Unfortunately, for a circumcised man, the pain is enhanced due to reduced cover. I was 8 days old when that happened, and Ice Swimming wasn't a consideration at the time. The only way is the grab the bucket of warm water, ask the girls to turn around (as if there was anything to see) and pour it on your private parts with great relief. I know everyone wants to know so here it is – NO, it doesn't freeze or get damaged, it recovers 100% and what doesn't kill you makes you stronger!

I got out, went to get dressed and was ready to second Kieron and Ryan. During my swim, Kieron decided that we need to oversee each other swim, up close and personal. So Kieron and Ryan walked by the 25m poolside as I was swimming back and forth until I was done. I didn't see a thing aside from the inside of my soul in every stroke I took.

Ryan and Kieron were getting ready, seeing me doing a one km was a double-edged sword. Ram did it therefore so can we, but now they had no choice but to do it, else, they would need to settle down in Siberia.

I was out, cold but defrosted, in time to see Kieron and Ryan diving for their 1km. They swam together, and it was amazing the see the two frozen South African caps ploughing through the ice water like synchronized swimming. At this temperature, the water surface freezes with a thin layer of ice in seconds. So just like curling, a person on each side with a rake was breaking that thin ice ahead of the swimmers.

They were doing very well, air temp at -33c, bitterly cold and here we are swimming, that doesn't make any sense, yes we are all probably certified nutters. Before I knew it, they finished their swim and were rushed to recovery. Both empty eyes, blank look lost in their inner soul.

As worried as we were I must admit that the Russian recovery process was amazing. They looked after us covered with sweat nonstop. We felt very safe in their hands and it was by far the best recovery we had in all our ice swims.

DONE!!! Nothing can explain the sense of pride and euphoria after completing such an intimidating challenge.

Three months later I was invited to Murmansk which has become a second home to me over the years. I asked Kieron and Ryan if they are keen to join for an Ice Mile. Ryan replied, "definitely not!" and Kieron was "Maybe". So I invited Kieron to my office, next to the big world map and started to sell the possible epic swim deep in Arctic Russia. My persuasion worked and Kieron was in. When Ryan found out, Fomo has taken over and he asked to join us. My first Ice zero, an Ice mike in zero-degree water what later on lead to me starting the International Ice Swimming Association events and races which set the foundation for the Winter Olympic games… one day. But that's in the next book.

Chapter 20
The International Ice Swimming Association

With IISA flag, in Antarctica.

The ice has some magical beauty, it's like the gods painted the world in a clean and pure white blanket. Everything seems like a fairy tale. Then they start sculpturing in the ice, creating the magnificent gigantic sculpture all from ice, all unique and completely natural, untouched by humans. It's beautiful and has a deadly attraction to it. Be very careful or it will devour you and turn you into ICE. Don't be afraid, listen to it, understand it and respect it and it will look after you.

In 2009 when I arrived back from Zurich, I knew I want to continue exploring the ICE and educate others by swimming in the icy waters about safety and integrity. My background is analytical and science. I believe in facts but I also believe in the immense strength of the mind. I was never a strong fit person. On the contrary. I struggled most of my youth trying to match up to the strong fit guys around me. I discovered I had a strong mind that can take me, sometimes, much further. I also had enough of pub stories and unsubstantiated achievements. I believe that sport has a very simple way of sorting the bullshit from reality and extreme sports do it even better. Let your actions do the talking. I knew I wanted to build a foundation for swimming in icy waters. I felt that I have just scratched some surface and seen something.

IISA South Africa event in Lesotho Mountains

The previous swims I have done set some boundaries. I knew that 1000m is very possible with some training and 2km plus will limit the sport to very few. So, I settled on 1 mile. I assumed an average time of 25 to 30 minutes in the water which was hard enough but between the impossible to possible. It all depends on your training, speed, fitness and all required.

I like to do things properly. So I set down and started to chart rules to set a foundation for the sport. The water temperature was set at 5C°. It was simple, clear and cold enough. It took me a few months to complete a constitution, rules, and structure. I had no idea where to go with this, but the term Ice Swimming (which is now used for ice dipping) was coined. So did the Ice

Mile, and many other terms that have become part of the jargon of this new sport.

I launched it in July 2009 and invited my swimming mates to join the first board. I needed some support. Later I restructured the board and took it from a Cape Town-based sport to a fully-fledged international sport.

Later on, in 2014 I created the 1km swimming event to channel the human competitive spirit from distance to speed. I clearly recall that board meeting when I introduced it and we all pondered what it will be like adding racing anxiety, speed and adrenaline to an already very extreme sport. We now allow for all distances from 50m to 1000m races.

We have Ice Swimming members from 78 countries around the world. 422 swimmers have completed an Ice Mile from 39 countries. We have avid swimmers from South Africa, Australia, New Zealand, India, South America and of course North America Europe and Asia. The sport is growing rapidly and We are in the process of discussions to take it to the Winter Olympic Games. The dream about the Olympic games started years ago and every year I grow more confident in our dream. We learnt so much and I still believe we are scratching the surface with Cold.

Ice Swimming has an impact on many other dimensions. It thought many of us about cold water and allowed us to recalibrate the concept of cold water and what is possible. Nowadays the North (Irish) Channel is fully booked every season (and Sarah Thoams just swam a double North Chanel in 22h at 12C°). A few years back it was a domain of the impossible. It allowed normal "average" people to discover the superhuman within and get out there and do some amazing fits that changed their lives for the better.

The International Ice Swimming Association ("IISA") was born.

Welcome to our mad world of ice swimming.

1. One mile or more in the water of 5°C or less.
2. One per standard swimming costume.
3. One pair of swimming goggles.

4. One silicon cap.
5. Nothing else, just swim, unassisted.
6. Safety plan, medical checks, support boats and team.
7. Be one with life's most deadly beauty and come back.

Ice Swimming has evolved and continues to do so. It's a story that changed my life and took me to the most remote places around the world. Meeting ordinary people with extraordinary capabilities. It enhanced my passion for nature, its rawness and its beauty. The beauty of the frozen parts of our world and for the people who actually live there, normal life.

I am 64 years old now and I am looking forward to the next icy adventure and continue to live life as if will be over tomorrow.

See you all in the ICE ...
or maybe another book... or Ice Swimming Olympic games...